# Her Mast

i

Wensleydale

*Flagged causey near Hardraw.*

# Her Master's Walks in Wensleydale

Stephen I. Robinson

bp
BARLEY • PUBLISHING
2007

Barley Publishing
10 Mill Green View
Swarcliffe
Leeds LS14 5JT
www.hm-walks.co.uk

First published 1994
Revised 2007



ISBN 1 898550 08 5. 2nd revised edition
(ISBN 1 898550 01 8. 1st edition)

Drawings by Andrew Haddelsey
Maps and photographs by Stephen I. Robinson



Printed in Great Britain by:
Aspire Print Solutions Ltd
Unit 9, Enterprise Court,
Pit Lane, Garforth, Leeds LS25 4BU
Telephone 0113 287 5141

*Cotterdale.*

# Contents

# Paw-word

**When I took over as custodian for these books I thought it would be an easy job. But walking with the master can be very worrying. Has he packed our snacks? When are we going to eat? Does he know where we are going? *I sometimes wonder!***

My mother warned me about him. She said 'Ringo,' – *that's me* – 'you've taken on a relentless task and will need to keep your wits about you. The master's opinion of an obvious track is certainly different from mine. I've often seen him knee-deep in mud muttering "?*$#*! Stupid rights of way !!!" Now if he'd followed me, he would have stayed clean and dry'.

Things are going to change now that I'm in command, I can tell you. My mother may have put up with his odd behaviour, but I don't see why I should. On the other hand, he does carry all the food, so it may be wiser to let him think he's in charge. I'll just give him a good firm tug now and then, that should keep him moving in the right direction.

We often walk for miles with nothing but the bleating of sheep or the call of the wild birds to disturb the silence, with no sign of humans, *unless you include the master.* If we do meet other walkers along the way they're nearly always friendly and stop to pass the time of day with us. Sometimes they make witty comments such as 'who's taking who for a walk?' Ha, ha, ha, if only I had a bonio for every time I've heard that one, I would be a very wealthy dog.

We both enjoy the peace and quiet of the countryside until, inspired by the beautiful landscape, the master decides to give a commentary .... *yawn, yawn, zzzzzzzzzz.* I'm so glad that my lead extends to 16 feet!

# Introduction

**Every year many thousands of visitors are attracted to the area contained within the Yorkshire Dales National Park. The estimated 1100 miles (1770km) of public footpaths and bridleways within the park provide some of the best walking in England.**

The fascinating and distinctive landscape of the Yorkshire Dales evolved over millions of years. Weathering of limestone, millstone grit, sandstone and shale, deposited about 300 million years ago, moulded the scenery that can be seen today. Man has also made his mark on the landscape through woodland clearances, cultivation of crops, sheep farming, establishing villages and building roads. The patchwork of fields, dry stone walls and isolated field barns are features unique to the Dales.

Wensleydale is the largest of all the Yorkshire Dales. It is a green and fertile valley, with many natural and man-made features. Its rich blend of limestone scars, wild moorland and green pastures contrasts dramatically with its swiftly flowing rivers and plunging waterfalls. Unlike the other major dales, Wensleydale is named after the village of Wensley and not its river, although it was once called Yoredale, from which the river Ure derives its name. The river Ure rises on Lunds Fell, close to the border of Yorkshire and Cumbria.

Carving its way confidently through the very heart of the Yorkshire Dales, this broad, U-shaped valley is joined by many tributary valleys, each contributing its own unique character. The remote Cotterdale has a spectacular waterfall; Raydale has a glacial lake; peaceful Bishopdale is green and fertile; isolated Walden is steep and narrow; secluded Coverdale is famed for its racehorses.

Painters, poets and writers have been inspired by Wensleydale's scenic beauty. Turner, the artist, made hundreds of drawings of the area between 1797 and 1831 for his grand *Histories of Yorkshire and Durham*. The Reverend Charles Kingsley visited the Dale in 1858. He commented, 'The richest spot in all England is this beautiful oasis in the mountains.'

The historian will find Wensleydale abundant in riches. Bronze Age settlers arrived about 2000 BC, introducing the use of metal and pottery. Iron Age Celts were next, establishing their field system of farming. The Romans constructed their long straight roads across the fells. Norse invaders cleared woodland and began the cultivation of the upper dales. The Anglo-Saxons were responsible for the large village greens. In the eleventh century the Normans arrived, building castles to establish their authority and setting aside huge areas as hunting forests. Later, Middleham Castle became the favourite home of Richard III and Bolton Castle a prison for Mary, Queen of Scots.

This cherished landscape is under close supervision by the National Park Authority. They have been charged with two prime objectives; 'to preserve and enhance the natural beauty of the area for the enjoyment of future generations' and 'to promote opportunities for a variety of outdoor recreation.' Traditional farming methods are encouraged and support is given for the conservation of natural habitats. This attracts a great variety of flora and fauna to the area.

We can all make a contribution to the protection of this beautiful and unique landscape. During your visit please follow the country code, and when it is time for you to depart, 'take nothing away but photographs and leave nothing behind except footsteps.'

*Stephen I. Robinson,*
*May 2007*

# Be Prepared!

**Walking, arguably the most enjoyable of outdoor pastimes and undoubtedly one of the healthiest, can be tailored to meet the requirements of almost anyone.**

Your preference might be for a gentle stroll of three to four miles along a quiet riverbank or woodland path, or perhaps a strenuous hill walk of ten miles or more. Whichever you choose, provided you are properly equipped, your walk will not only be safer but also more enjoyable. This does not mean taking everything including the kitchen sink! If you are a keen photographer a camera with spare films or memory card is essential. The artist needs his sketchbook and pencil. Binoculars are mandatory for birdwatchers. But please remember, everything you take is extra weight to be carried.

What to wear and carry will depend on the season, the weather and good sense.

The items in the following lists are recommended, but think carefully about what to take. Some extra items may be needed on a hill walk which could be left behind when walking through the lower meadows. Due to our unpredictable climate, however, a spare wool sweater and waterproofs should always be carried. *(Items in italics could be used in warmer conditions.)*

**TO WEAR**

Strong walking boots or stout shoes
Thick woollen socks (two pairs)
Cotton shirt *or T-Shirt*
Walking breeches, trousers *or shorts*
(Jeans are not advisable, they lose their heat retention when wet)
Woollen hat, balaclava *or sun hat*

**TO CARRY**

A small rucksack, thirty to forty litres in capacity, to carry the following:
Waterproof anorak or cagoule
Wool sweater or fibre pile jacket
Small hand towel or baby wipes
Gloves, scarf
First aid kit, compass, whistle
Torch, pencil and note pad
Ordnance Survey map of the area
Emergency rations, survival bag
Water bottle with water
Food and snacks

**OPTIONAL ITEMS**

Camera and spare films or memory card
binoculars
Swiss army knife
Flask with tea, coffee, soup or
other hot drink
Waterproof over-trousers, gaiters
Five to ten yards (or metres) of thin cord
(Useful for temporary laces etc.)

*Semer Water.*

# About the Walks

**The walks explore some of the most spectacular and beautiful countryside, providing a wide variety of scenery; limestone scars, lush meadows, woodland, sparkling rivers and waterfalls.**

All of the walks follow circular routes ranging from 5½ to 9½ miles (8.8 to 15.3km). They begin from a public car park where one is available, or at a place where it is possible to park safely without blocking farm gateways or causing inconvenience to others.

For this edition all of the routes were resurveyed between August and November 2006 and the maps have been amended where necessary. However, from time to time walls, fences and hedges may be removed, stiles and gates resited, new forestry established and buildings could be demolished. For this reason it is recommended that the relevant Ordnance Survey maps and a compass are carried. These will help to determine landmarks and locate alternative routes where necessary.

The relevant area of the map has been used and then simplified so that only the walls, fences, buildings, rivers, roads and landmarks etc where the route passes through are included.

Each map has the route marked in red with numbered arrow pointers for each section of the route. These relate to the descriptive guide on the facing page, which includes a grid reference for each stage of the walk. When used together these features should help to avoid confusion, but common sense and some map reading experience are desirable.

The times given for completion of the walks are approximate and do not include any allowance for lunch breaks, photo stops or sightseeing. As a rule of thumb, adding one third of the stated time for stops should be sufficient. If accompanied by young children extra walking time will have to be allowed. Extended stays at any of the inns or tea shops *en route* should also be added to the time.

# WEST BURTON and THE TEMPLARS' CHAPEL

## FROM AYSGARTH 6¾ MILES (10.8KM)

**This scenic walk begins with a visit to the famous Aysgarth Falls and continues into the beautiful side valley of Bishopdale. The views are fabulous and apart from one steep climb the walking is easy.**

Aysgarth is probably most famous for its waterfalls, which are seen at their best after heavy rain. In less than a mile the river Ure plunges 200 feet (60m) over three spectacular falls. The upper fall was featured in the film *Robin Hood, Prince of Thieves* starring Kevin Costner as Robin. He was seen fighting against Little John as he tried to ford the river.

Our route from the car park leads across the river to Yore Mill, a large four-storey building which has seen a variety of uses over the years. It was built in 1784 as a cotton mill. After a fire in 1852 it was rebuilt and changed to wool spinning. The mill supplied the material that was used to make the 'red shirts' for Garibaldi's revolutionary army in Italy. It operated as a flour mill from 1912 to 1958 and became home to the Yorkshire Carriage Museum in 1969, housing one of Britain's largest collections of carriages and horse-drawn vehicles. Sadly, the museum closed down in 2001 and all of the carriages were auctioned off. However, Yore Mill is still open to the public and remains worthy of a visit.

From the mill a flight of steps leads to the imposing St Andrew's Church. In the twelfth century, Aysgarth was England's largest parish with more than 81,000 acres (32,800ha) and covered all of Upper Wensleydale. Most of the present church was rebuilt in 1866, but the bell tower dates from the fourteenth century and has a peal of six bells. The finely carved rood screen and the abbot's stall were rescued from Jervaulx Abbey after the dissolution of the monasteries.

After leaving the churchyard we follow a meadow path to Eshington Bridge and then continue along the fertile valley floor of Bishopdale to West Burton. Bishopdale is the largest of the many tributaries draining into Wensleydale. It has a deep U-shape which indicates that it was formed by glacial action.

West Burton is an enchanting, old-fashioned village, standing at the junction of Bishopdale and Walden. It has a large sloping green, market cross and stocks. At the lower end of the green a path leads to an ancient packhorse bridge which crosses Walden Beck. Cauldron Falls can be seen further upstream. It is possible to get quite close to the falls which plunge into a shallow pool shaded by trees.

From the bridge our path leads uphill through Barrack Wood to Hudson Lane, where a wonderful panorama unfolds. Walden, Bishopdale and Wensleydale are seen in a single sweep. Buckden Pike rises behind Walden Moor, the craggy outcrops of Kidstones Scar stand out at the head of Bishopdale and looking across the main Wensleydale valley the villages of Aysgarth, Carperby, Castle Bolton and Redmire are clearly visible.

We continue along the slopes of Penhill to join High Lane, once a busy drove road linking Bishopdale to Middleham. Cattle and sheep were herded along this track in their thousands. From High Lane our route leads to the Templars' Chapel.

The Order of the Poor Knights of the Temple of Solomon, better known as the Knights Templars or The Temple, was founded early in the twelfth century and introduced to Britain in 1146. Its purpose was to protect pilgrims travelling to and from Jerusalem. The order acquired land on Penhill to build a chapel and dedicated it to 'God, the Virgin and St Catherine.' St Catherine, the patron saint of linen weavers, was important to the Templars because their outer garments were made of white linen on which was sewn a blood red cross, their symbol of martyrdom.

The order acquired immense wealth and political power and it was this which caused their downfall. Kings and Popes alike grew jealous of their influence, and they were subjected to much persecution. Pope Clement V abolished the order in 1312, Edward II having seized all the property of the English Templars in 1308. Many of the Templars were imprisoned and some were tortured and executed.

Leaving the chapel we descend to the main road which is followed to Hestholme Bridge. Here a meadow path entices us away and delivers us to the banks of the river Ure where we continue upstream returning to the churchyard at Aysgarth.

| | |
|---|---|
| **Start/Parking:** | Car park at Aysgarth Falls National Park Visitor Centre. |
| **Location:** | Aysgarth Falls is situated 8 miles (12.8km) west of Leyburn on the A684 Northallerton to Sedburgh road. |
| **Grid Ref:** | SE 011 887. |
| **Distance:** | 6¾ miles (10.8km) circular. Allow 3½ hrs walking time. |
| **Total Ascent:** | 1152 feet (351m) Maximum Elevation: 1148 feet (349m). |
| **OS Maps:** | Explorer OL30 (1:25,000) or Landranger 98 (1:50,000). |
| **Refreshments:** | The National Park Visitor Centre, the Palmer Flatts Hotel, the George and Dragon Inn, Mill Race Tea Shop and Kitty's Tea Rooms at Aysgarth. |
| | The Fox and Hounds at West Burton. |
| **Public Toilets:** | National Park Visitor Centre. |
| **Other:** | Post Office, telephone, bus service, Edwardian Rock Garden. |

Cauldron Falls at West Burton

| | |
|---|---|
| Cairn/Hilltop | Route |
| Building | River/Stream |
| Ruin | Crag/Scar |
| Woodland | A or B Road |
| Miles walked | Minor Road |
| Viewpoint | Unfenced Road |
| Car Park (Pay) | Farm Road or Cart Track |
| Other Parking | |



## AYSGARTH FALLS

To visit the middle and lower falls first, follow the track from the car park entrance. The route is well signposted and the track is good. After viewing the falls return to the car park and follow the route as described.

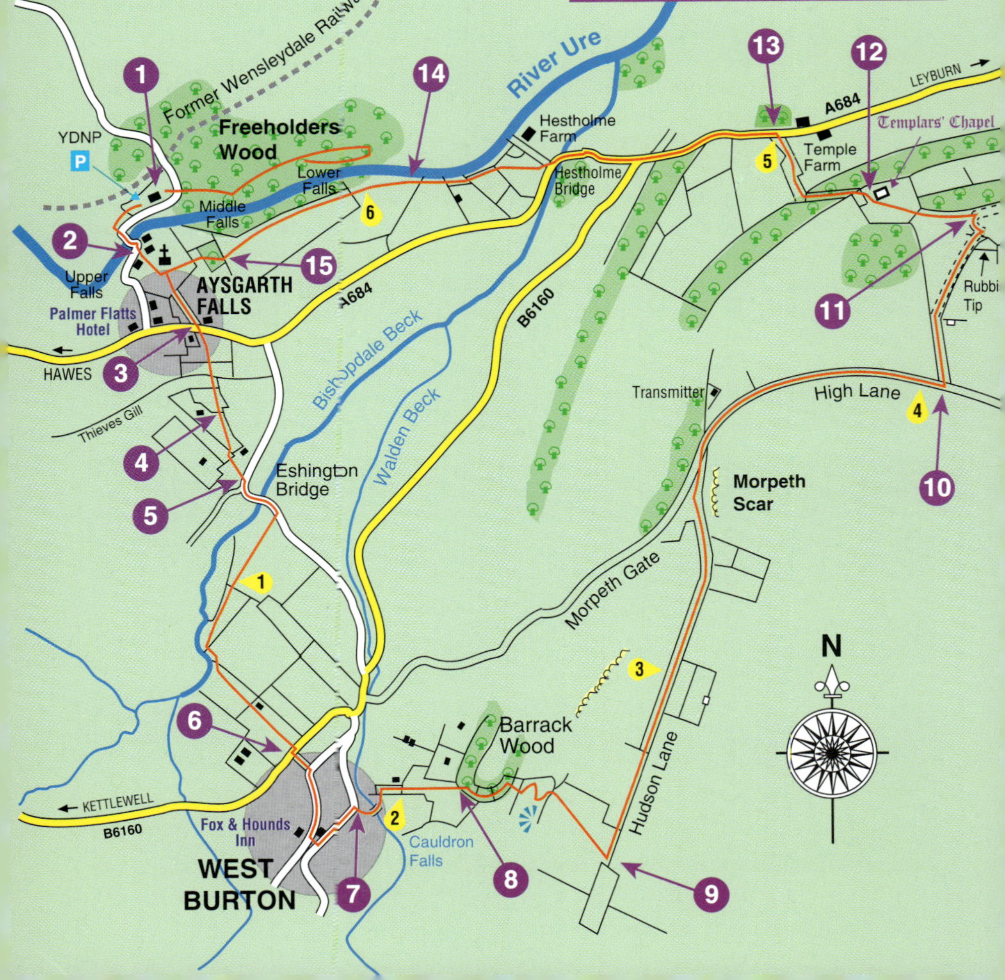

(APRIL 16) NICE WALK NOT TOO HARD

# West Burton and the Templars' Chapel

**1** *(GR 011 887)* Leave the car park at the opposite end to the entrance *(SP Upper Falls)* follow the path down to the road and continue across the bridge.

**2** *(GR 011 886)* Leave the road *(Sign St Andrew's Church)*. Climb some steps, go through a gate and follow the path to the front of the church. With your back to the church door follow a path leading directly away from the church. Leave the churchyard via a gate and follow a tarmac lane to the main A684 road.

**3** *(GR 013 883)* Cross the road and go through the gap-stile opposite *(SP Eshington Bridge)*. Cross the field and go through another gap-stile. Descend to a wooden step-stile in the valley bottom *(Thieves Gill)*, then follow the fence up and go through a gated stile. Bear right slightly and descend through a gate at the bottom of the field.

**4** *(GR 014 880)* Continue downhill and go through a stile in the bottom right corner of the field. After about 15 yards (13m) go through a stile on the left and then head down to stile leading onto the road.

**5** *(GR 015 878)* Turn right and follow the road. After crossing Eshington Bridge leave the road via a gap-stile on the right *(SP West Burton)*. Cross the field and go over a wooden step-stile. Follow the right wall to its end. Bear left to go through two stiles by the side of Bishopdale Beck. Continue on a clear path through two fields to reach the road.

**6** *(GR 016 869)* Cross the road and climb the steps opposite *(SP West Burton 75yds)*. Follow an enclosed track to a gap-stile leading onto the road. Turn right and follow the road to the village centre passing the Fox and Hounds. At the road junction turn left and follow the road past the village cross and stocks to the bottom of the green.

**7** *(GR 018 867)* Turn right onto a rough track *(SP Morpeth Gate and Cote Bridge)*. Cross a stone packhorse bridge. After a few yards turn left and follow a stepped path up to a stile. Go through the stile, turn right and continue uphill. Go through a stile by a barn, bear half left and climb towards Barrack Wood.

**8** *(GR 022 868)* Enter the wood over a wooden step-stile, turn right *(SP Hudson Quarry Lane)* and continue on a clear path through two stiles to leave the wood. Climb steeply through two pastures, then bear half right climbing steadily up to a wall.

**9** *(GR 027 865)* Turn left *(SP Morpeth Scar)* onto Hudson Lane following the shoulder of Penhill. At a junction *(near Morpeth Scar)* turn right and continue along a rough stone track *(High Lane)*. Follow the track to a T-Junction.

**10** *(GR 038 881)* Go through the gate on the left and follow an enclosed track. The track soon opens out and becomes a concrete surface as it begins to descend.

**11** *(GR 039 887)* On the second part of a double bend, turn left and leave the track. Descend between two woods, go through a gate and then bear right descending towards a fenced enclosure *(The Templars' Chapel)*.

**12** *(GR 035 888)* Go through a gap-stile *(SP Temple Farm)*. Turn right and descend a stony track. At the bottom go through a gate, turn right and follow the wall past Temple Farm. Bear left and go through a gap-stile onto the main A684 road.

**13** *(GR 032 890)* Turn left and follow the road. After crossing Hestholme Bridge, go through a gate at the entrance to Hestholme Farm. Head diagonally across the field to reach the riverside. Continue through three fields following the river upstream.

**14** *(GR 021 888)* Leave the riverbank and follow an obvious track climbing alongside a wood. Go through a stile and gate combination and continue close to the wood. When the boundaries of the field become clear, bear left towards a small wood.

**15** *(GR 014 886)* Cross a wooden step-stile and continue on a clear path through the wood. Leave the wood via another wooden step-stile, *(Aysgarth Church comes into view)* cross the field to a gated stile leading into the churchyard. Continue to the church entrance and follow the outward route back to the car park.

# CARPERBY and CASTLE BOLTON

## FROM AYSGARTH 10¼ MILES (16.5KM)

**From the outset, this delightful walk allows the rich and varied scenery of Wensleydale to be enjoyed at its best. The gradients are gentle, the paths are easy to follow and the views are outstanding.**

Aysgarth's National Park Centre and the adjoining buildings were originally cottages belonging to the Wensleydale Railway. The line opened in 1878 linking Leyburn with Hawes, a branch line to Garsdale also linked with the Settle and Carlisle line. It provided comfortable travel for visitors to the dale. Goods trains transported farm produce, livestock, milk and stone out of the dale, returning with coal, food, clothes and other goods. The line closed in 1954 and the track between Garsdale and Redmire was removed in 1965. Enthusiasts have been campaigning for many years to reopen the railway.

After leaving the car park we follow a clear path through Freeholders' Wood and lush meadows to Carperby.

Carperby is an attractive village with most of its cottages straddling the road. It was granted a market charter in 1305, although the market cross is dated 1674. In the seventeenth century the village became a centre for Quakerism and its largest building is the former Friends' Meeting House built in 1864. There is a tradition that any person 'who put up a smoke' in Carperby had sporting rights in Freeholders' Wood and also the right to collect wood from October to March; the latter part of this tradition, known as 'estovers', is still upheld today.

From Carperby we follow a waymarked path to Castle Bolton. Sited high on the hillside, the large village green is lined by cottages built on two levels and all facing south. The church of St Oswald, built in 1325, has a sundial on the porch which has been in permanent shadow since the building of Bolton Castle.

Bolton Castle was built by Richard, Lord Scrope, Chancellor of England. The work began in 1379 and took more than eighteen years to complete at a cost of £12,000. Mary, Queen of Scots, was held here in 'honourable custody' after her defeat at Langside in May 1568. Her stay at Bolton Castle lasted until January 1569, when she was moved to Tutbury. Mary spent the next eighteen years imprisoned in one castle after another before she was beheaded at Fotheringhay Castle.

In 1644, after the battle of Marston Moor, the castle was besieged for over a year by the Parliamentary Forces. Before they surrendered, the Royalists had been reduced to eating their own horses.

Our route from the castle leads to the higher pastures, where there are extensive views across Wensleydale. The prominent bulk of Penhill rises from its woodland terraces and to the east a clear day extends the view to the North York Moors. The beautiful side valleys of Bishopdale and Walden, lying to the right of Penhill, wind their way south separated by Wasset Fell.

On reaching Ox Close Pasture, below the limestone cliffs of Ivy Scar, there are remains of a Bronze Age stone circle. This is the largest stone circle in the Yorkshire Dales, measuring about 90 feet (27m) across, and it is believed to have had a sacred purpose.

We continue past the striking waterfall of Disher Force and then descend to the hamlet of Woodhall. From here our route leads to an area known as Rabbit Warren. This large man-made rabbit warren was established in the 1750s by Thomas Metcalfe. It was used for breeding silver-haired rabbits whose skins were in great demand until the early 1800s. Rabbit fur returned to fashion in the early twentieth century and was used to line the luxurious motoring coats of the Edwardian period. Tzar Nicholas II is reputed to have been a patron.

The hill with the crest of pine trees is Lady Hill. During the ice age a debris of clay, sand and rocks was carried along by the glaciers. As the ice melted this was dropped into heaps. The pressure of the ice moving over these deposits moulded them into oval shaped hillocks known as drumlins, of which Lady Hill is a fine example.

During our return to Aysgarth we pass Bear Park. The name may be a corruption of Beaurepaire which means 'the beautiful retreat'. Built into the north wall of the house is a carved tombstone, brought from Coverham Abbey. We continue past Aysgarth's Upper Falls and then return to the car park.

| | |
|---|---|
| **Start/Parking:** | Car park at Aysgarth Falls National Park Visitor Centre. |
| **Location:** | Aysgarth Falls is situated 8 miles (12.8km) west of Leyburn on the A684 Northallerton to Sedburgh road. |
| **Grid Ref:** | SE 011 887. |
| **Distance:** | 10¼ miles (16.5km) circular. Allow 5 hrs walking time. |
| **Total Ascent:** | 1646 feet (508m) Maximum Elevation: 1091 feet (333m). |
| **OS Maps:** | Explorer OL30 (1:25,000) or Landranger 98 (1:50,000). |
| **Refreshments:** | The National Park Visitor Centre, the Palmer Flatts Hotel, the George and Dragon Inn, Mill Race Tea Shop and Kitty's Tea Rooms at Aysgarth.<br>The Wheatsheaf Hotel at Carperby. |
| **Public Toilets:** | National Park Visitor Centre and Castle Bolton. |
| **Other:** | Post Office, telephone, bus service, Edwardian Rock Garden. |

CASTLE BOLTON
Bolton Castle
Castle Bank
Intake Plantation
West Bolton
Beldon Beck
Strip Lynchets
Angelhaw Hill
West Gill
Ford
Strip Lynchets
Low Gate
Locker Tarn
Peatmoor Lane
New Pasture
Ox Close
Enclosure
IVY SCAR
Old Lead mines
Ford
Disher Force
Garage
WOODHALL
Ellers Beck
Ballowfield
Rabbit Warren
LADY HILL
A684
HAWES
Harper Wath Footbridge
River Ure
AYSGARTH
George & Dragon Inn
Upper Falls
Palmer Flatts Hotel
AYSGARTH FALLS
Middle Falls
Lower Falls
Freeholders' Wood
Former Station
Low Lane
Bear Park
CARPERBY
The Wheatsheaf Inn
East End Farm
Route of former Wensleydale Railway Line
REDMIRE LEYBURN
LEYBURN
Cairn/Hilltop
Building
Ruin
Woodland
Miles walked
Viewpoint
Car Park (Pay)
Other Parking
Route
River/Stream
Crag/Scar
A or B Road
Minor Road
Unfenced Road
Farm Road or Cart Track
Reproduced by permission of Ordnance Survey on behalf of The Controller of Her Majesty's Stationery Office, © Crown Copyright 100016545.

# Carperby and Castle Bolton

**1** *(GR 011 887)* From the car park entrance, turn left and follow the road under a bridge. Leave the road via a gate on the right *(SP Carperby Village 1m)* leading into Freeholders' Wood. After crossing another track leave the wood via a gap-stile. Follow a clear route through four more gap-stiles. Turn left and go through a gap-stile leading onto a farm lane.

**2** *(GR 011 895)* Go through the stile opposite *(SP Carperby Village)* and continue in line with the right wall across the field. Follow the right wall to a barn and then bear left towards the far left corner of the field. Go through a stile, turn right *(SP Carperby)* and continue through another stile which leads into Carperby.

**3** *(GR 008 899)* Turn right and follow the road past the Wheatsheaf Inn. Near the end of the village go through a stile on the left *(SP Castle Bolton 1¾)*, turn right at a barn and follow a farm track uphill. Continue along the track and go through a broken wall.

**4** *(GR 014 904)* Continue via three gap-stiles and head to the left side of the wood *(West Bolton Plantation)*. Cross a stream, follow a derelict wall uphill and go through a gate. Continue via two gap-stiles to West Bolton Farm.

**5** *(GR 020 909)* Pass to the right of the farm and go through a gate. Continue through two more gap-stiles, now descend into a gully to cross the footbridge over Beldon Beck. Climb back up from the gully and go through a gap-stile.

**6** *(GR 026 913)* Continue to a wall corner, bear left and cross the next field by two wooden step-stiles. Head towards a small wood by the castle. At a signpost *(Castle Bolton)* go through two more gap-stiles and a gate to enter Castle Bolton.

**7** *(GR 033 919)* After visiting the village and the castle, return to this point. Follow a clear track through eight gates to its end.

**8** *(GR 014 919)* After the eighth gate turn left *(SP Carperby)* and follow a rutted track, keeping with the wall to its corner. Continue straight ahead, cross Beldon Beck via a ford and climb uphill to a gate.

**9** *(GR 009 917)* Go through the gate into a rough pasture and continue along a broad green path which is waymarked in places.

**10** *(GR 007 909)* Leave the pasture via a gate and take the right fork *(SP Askrigg 5)*, heading uphill away from the left wall. After crossing a farm lane *(Peatmoor Lane)*, go through a stile and follow a clear path leading through several pastures.

**11** *(GR 994 903)* After passing a large sheepfold go through a gate into Ox Close Pasture and descend gradually to pass below Ivy Scar and some old lead mine workings. Join a wide track from the mines and follow it through a gate to a stream *(Disher Force)*.

**12** *(GR 981 904)* Ford the stream, turn left and follow the track through two gates. Descend steeply on a stony track via two more gates to the main road at Woodhall.

**13** *(GR 977 903)* Turn left and cross the road, go through a gap-stile in the wall corner opposite the garage *(SP Ballowfield 1)*. Follow the left wall and cross a ladder-stile. Bear right through the area known as Rabbit Warren and descend to cross a step-stile in the fence. Turn left and go through a gap-stile, continue via four more stiles returning to the main road.

**14** *(GR 992 893)* Turn right onto the road, at a T-junction turn right *(SP Aysgarth Via Yore Bridge)*. After about 100 yards (91m) go through a gate on the left *(SP Aysgarth Falls)* climb some steps to join the old railway line, follow this over a bridge and a wooden stile.

**15** *(GR 999 891)* At a fence the path is diverted left to pass through a broken wall and a gap-stile. Follow the wall round to the right and go through a gap-stile. Continue along the right wall/fence through two more gap-stiles to reach the farm lane at Bear Park.

**16** *(GR 006 889)* Cross the farm lane, climb a stone step-stile and keep to the left of the farm. Go through a gap-stile, turn right passing a tennis court and go through another gap-stile *(SP Aysgarth)*. Follow two waymark posts across a farm track and descend to the right.

**17** *(GR 008 887)* Go over a stile by a gate and pass between the stone supports of an old railway bridge. Turn left and follow a clear fenced path, passing the entrance to the Upper Falls and continue down to the bridge. Go through the left gate joining a path which leads into the bottom end of the National Park Visitor Centre car park.

# 3

# SEMER WATER and the RIVER BAIN

## FROM BAINBRIDGE 8¾ MILES (14KM)

**This enchanting walk is enriched with some of the finest scenery in Upper Wensleydale. There are a few steep climbs, but these are amply rewarded with splendid views. A Roman road and a former glacial lake are among the many interesting features to enjoy.**

Bainbridge is a most attractive village set in the very heart of Wensleydale. It has a large village green enclosed by fine stone houses and the prominently placed Rose and Crown Hotel. The hotel, often referred to as the 'Pride of Wensleydale', dates from 1445 and is the custodian of the Bainbridge forest horn. In medieval times a horn was blown at Bainbridge to guide travellers to the safety of the village. During the winter months, from the Feast of Holy Rood, 27th September, to Shrove Tuesday the horn was blown at 9pm each evening. The duty of the hornblower was carried out by various members of the Metcalfe family for more than a century. In the 1950s Jack Metcalfe could reach and maintain a top C note for up seven seconds which could be heard three miles away. This custom continued until recent times, but nowadays the horn is only sounded on special occasions.

Our route from the village follows the Cam High Road, a Roman road which once connected the fort on Brough Hill with the military station at Ribchester in Lancashire. The views from this ancient road are spectacular. Sweeping right from the flat topped Yorburgh are Wild Boar Fell, Lunds Fell, Hugh Seat, Great Shunner Fell and Lovely Seat.

After leaving the Roman road we climb steeply over the ridge into the beautiful valley of Raydale. Our descent to Marsett provides excellent views of Semer Water.

Across the valley behind Stalling Busk another Roman road is visible. This leads over Stake Moss and into Wharfedale.

Both Marsett and Stalling Busk are small farming communities that are linked by a rough track, although in places a boat might be more appropriate than walking boots!

The church of St Matthew at Stalling Busk was built in 1909 and looks very much like a Swiss chalet. A short distance from the village we arrive at the former church. Originally built in 1603, it was rebuilt in 1722 on the same site. It had an unusual layout with the pews arranged around a central pulpit. It fell into disuse when the new church was built and was soon stripped of its roof and furnishings. The graveyard is still in use and provides a peaceful resting place looking across Semer Water.

Semer Water was created during the last ice age; as the glacier moved forward it scraped out the bed of the lake, pushing the debris to the foot of the valley. When the ice melted this debris was left behind forming a dam. The lake covers an area of about 65 acres (26ha) with a maximum depth of around 35 feet (11m).

Legend records a different origin for Semer Water associated with a sunken village. An angel disguised himself as a beggar and sought alms from house to house throughout the village. Turned away hungry, he arrived at a small cottage on the outskirts where he was fed and given shelter for the night. As he left the village on the following day, he looked back, discarded his beggar's clothes and exclaimed:

*Semer Water rise, Semer Water sink,*
*And cover all save yon little house,*
*That gave me meat and drink.*

The earth gaped, the lake rose and all perished except the inhabitants of the little house. Legend aside, when the level of the lake was lowered in 1937, evidence was found of Iron Age lakeside dwellings which could have been destroyed by the lake rising during a sudden flood.

Leaving the lake we follow England's shortest river, the Bain, almost its full course back to Bainbridge. As we descend there are superb views across Wensleydale and to the right of Bainbridge is the flat-topped Brough Hill. This was the site of a Roman fort called Virosidum. It was built in AD 80 by Julius Agricola during his campaign to suppress the Celtic tribes of Yorkshire. A garrison of 500 men was stationed at the fort which was occupied until AD 395.

From the bridge there is a good view of the crescent shaped Bain Falls, where the river Bain makes one final protest before merging with the river Ure downstream. Just over the bridge is Low Mill which has a restored waterwheel.

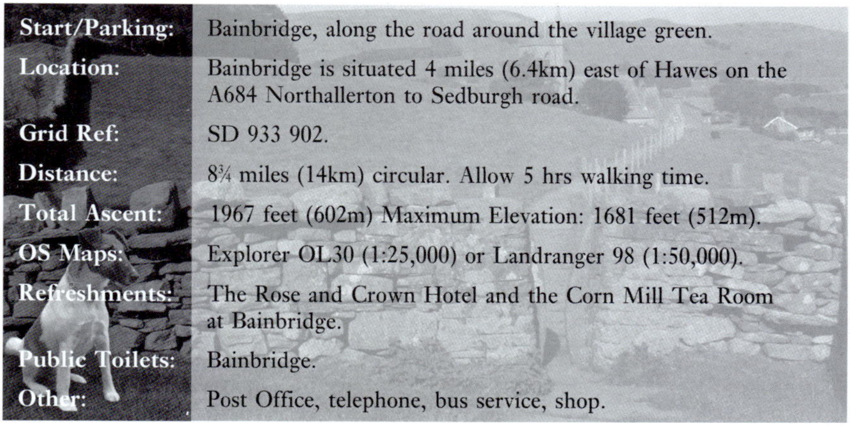

| | |
|---|---|
| **Start/Parking:** | Bainbridge, along the road around the village green. |
| **Location:** | Bainbridge is situated 4 miles (6.4km) east of Hawes on the A684 Northallerton to Sedburgh road. |
| **Grid Ref:** | SD 933 902. |
| **Distance:** | 8¾ miles (14km) circular. Allow 5 hrs walking time. |
| **Total Ascent:** | 1967 feet (602m) Maximum Elevation: 1681 feet (512m). |
| **OS Maps:** | Explorer OL30 (1:25,000) or Landranger 98 (1:50,000). |
| **Refreshments:** | The Rose and Crown Hotel and the Corn Mill Tea Room at Bainbridge. |
| **Public Toilets:** | Bainbridge. |
| **Other:** | Post Office, telephone, bus service, shop. |

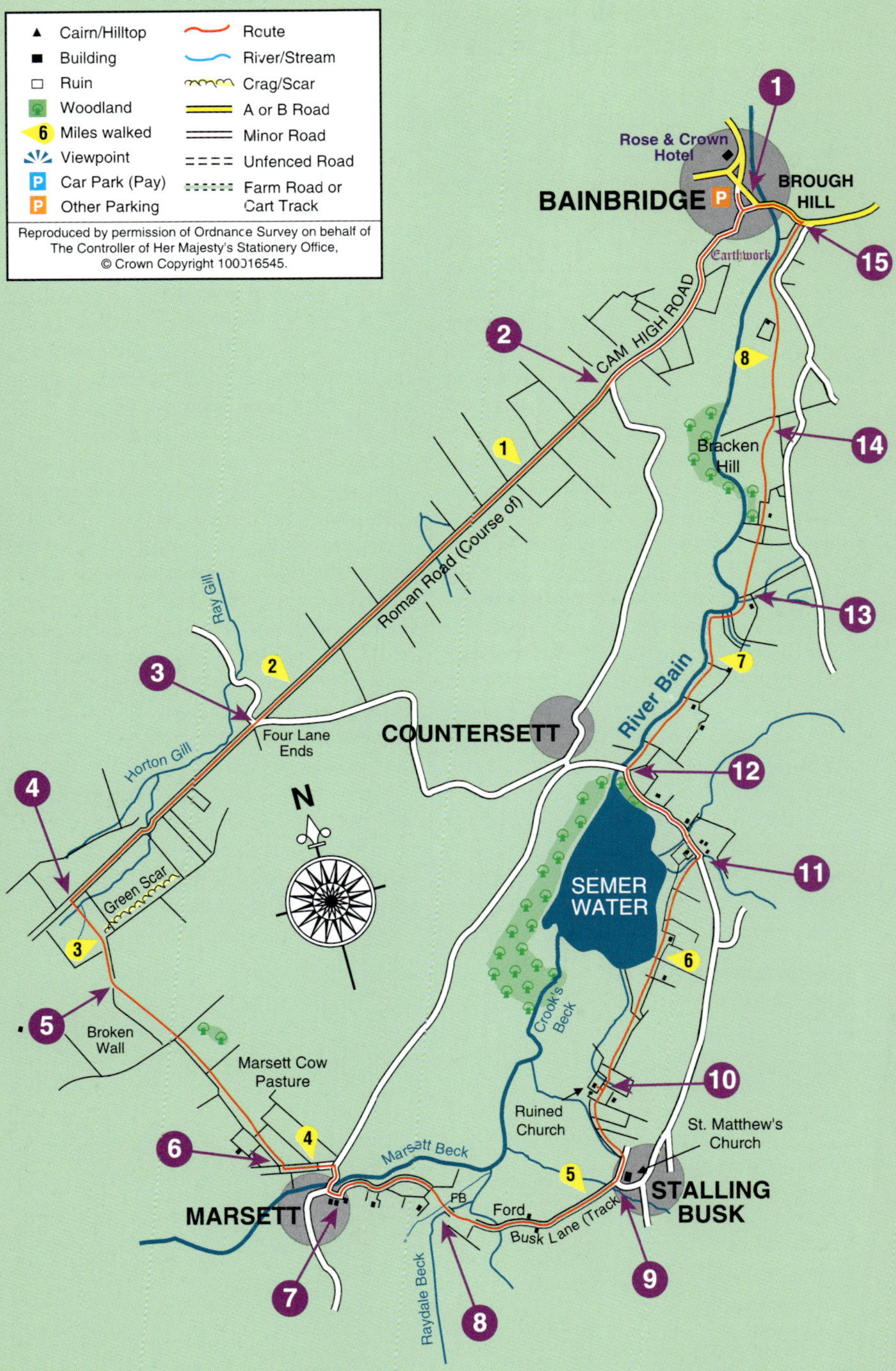

Cairn/Hilltop
Building
Ruin
Woodland
Miles walked
Viewpoint
Car Park (Pay)
Other Parking
Route
River/Stream
Crag/Scar
A or B Road
Minor Road
Unfenced Road
Farm Road or Cart Track
Reproduced by permission of Ordnance Survey on behalf of The Controller of Her Majesty's Stationery Office, © Crown Copyright 100016545.
Rose & Crown Hotel
BAINBRIDGE
BROUGH HILL
Earthwork
CAM HIGH ROAD
Roman Road (Course of)
Bracken Hill
Ray Gill
Four Lane Ends
COUNTERSETT
River Bain
Horton Gill
N
Green Scar
SEMER WATER
Broken Wall
Marsett Cow Pasture
Crook's Beck
Ruined Church
St. Matthew's Church
STALLING BUSK
Marsett Beck
MARSETT
FB
Ford
Busk Lane (Track)
Raydale Beck

# SEMER WATER AND THE RIVER BAIN

**1** *(GR 933 902)* Leave Bainbridge at the south side of the village green on the road signposted Countersett, Semer Water and Marsett, go past the Bainbridge Temperance Hall and begin a steady climb uphill.

**2** *(GR 925 895)* After approximately ¾ mile (1km) when the road bends left, leave the road and continue ahead on an enclosed track *(SP Byway Beggarmans Road 5½).*

**3** *(GR 905 884)* Cross a tarmacked road *(Four Lane Ends)* and continue climbing steadily along the enclosed track heading towards Yorburgh.

**4** *(GR 895 878)* After passing Green Scar go through a stile on the left *(SP Marsett).* Follow a clear track uphill and go through a gate. Continue alongside a limestone scar and a derelict wall.

**5** *(GR 896 874)* At a waymark post go through the wall and bear half right along a faint path, the route soon becomes clearer and descends in line with the right wall to a ladder-stile. *(There is also a dog gate at this stile!)* After crossing the stile, continue along the wall side descending steeply through three pastures. Go through a gate/stile leading onto a farm lane.

**6** *(GR 901 864)* Turn left and follow the farm lane down to the main road. Turn right towards Marsett, cross the bridge and turn left heading towards a farm.

**7** *(GR 903 862)* Turn left *(SP Semer Water and Stalling Busk)* and continue alongside Marsett Beck to join an enclosed lane. At the end of this lane go through a gate and continue across the field towards a footbridge.

**8** *(GR 908 860)* Cross the footbridge and head towards another footbridge. Pass to the right of this bridge and join an enclosed lane *(Busk Lane)*. Cross a concrete ford and after going through a gate begin a steepish climb to the hamlet of Stalling Busk.

**9** *(GR 916 859)* Turn left and go past the church. Leave the road at a signpost on the left *(SP Ruined Church)*. Pass through a gap-stile and two gates to reach the ruined church. Enter the graveyard through a gap-stile.

**10** *(GR 916 863)* Leave the graveyard over the same stile and turn left. Continue through four stiles to reach the bank of Semer Water. Leave the lake through three gap-stiles and go over a ladder-stile onto the main road.

**11** *(GR 924 872)* Turn left and follow the road to the lake's outlet at Semer Water Bridge. *(Don't cross the bridge.)*

**12** *(GR 921 877)* Leave the road via a stile on the right *(SP Bainbridge)*. Follow the River Bain downstream through four fields and cross a footbridge. Continue along the riverside and at the field boundary bear right to cross a ladder-stile.

**13** *(GR 929 884)* Leave the riverbank and continue straight ahead, climbing up through three gap-stiles and then continue uphill to the summit of Bracken Hill.

**14** *(GR 932 891)* From the hilltop descend through a gap-stile and follow a clear green path passing to the right of a large walled enclosure. Head towards the right wall and follow it downhill towards Bain Falls.

**15** *(GR 936 900)* Go through the gap-stile, turn left and follow the road over the bridge and back to the village centre.

## THE CARLOW STONE

On the shoreline at Semer Water is a huge boulder known as the Carlow Stone that was supposedly thrown at the Devil by a giant *(see walk 4)*. Tradition has it that the stone was visited by courting couples when they became engaged. Touching the stone was said to bring good fortune - and, in due course, large and healthy families.

# 4

# ADDLEBROUGH and the CAUSEYS

## FROM THORNTON RUST 8 MILES (12.9KM)

**Starting from the ancient village of Thornton Rust this walk has an excellent mixture of terrain and scenery. It is a journey filled with legend and history. The views are exceptional.**

Thornton Rust, recorded as Torentun in Domesday Book, is an attractive and peaceful village well away from the heavy traffic passing through the valley bottom. Its history can be traced back to the fourth century when there was a small chapel dedicated to St Restitutus, a Bishop from London.

We leave the village along a walled lane meandering uphill onto the open moor and the slopes of Addlebrough. The hill is named after the British chief, Authulf, whose burial site is said to be marked by a cairn on its summit. Addlebrough may have been used as a lookout station by the Romans, who had a fort at Bainbridge.

Our route across Thornton Rust Moor traces the course of a glacial valley and on its southern slope is a large stone covered burial mound called Stony Raise. Despite stone robbing, excavations and mindless treasure hunters, it still covers an area of 113 feet (34.5m) and stands at a height of 8 feet (2.4m). Legend records that a giant fell here, dropping a heavy chest of gold. The chest fell to the ground, sank into the earth and was covered with stones. It is said that the chest will be recovered by a mortal when a fairy appears as an ape or a hen, but it must be removed in complete silence and without cursing!

At Carpley Green we continue along a quiet lane towards Bainbridge. There are good views of Semer Water with Wether Fell rising behind. To the north is the wild moorland of Askrigg Common which separates Wensleydale from Swaledale.

Bainbridge was established in the late twelfth century when it became the headquarters for the Wardens of the Forest of Wensleydale. They were entrusted with guarding the forest and its game in the King's name. The medieval stocks on the village green were in use during the reign of Elizabeth I. Offenders were fastened in the stocks for several days to be abused by other villagers, who would throw rubbish at them as a punishment

After crossing Yorebridge we reach the first of the flagged causeys. The causeys were built in the eighteenth century to provide a dryer route to the market and mills at Askrigg. Our path leads to the tiny hamlet of Grange. This was the site of Fors Abbey, founded as a Savigniac monastery in 1145 and absorbed into the Cistercian order in 1147. The monks toiled for eleven years to establish their abbey. However, the harsh climate and rough land eventually forced them to move to the more hospitable site at Jervaulx in 1156. The abbey continued to be used as a chantry chapel and grange farm until the dissolution.

From Grange we follow another causey to Mill Gill. In 1908 a local entrepreneur, William Handley Burton, harnessed the power of Mill Gill to generate electricity for Askrigg. He devised similar schemes for other villages in Wensleydale and Swaledale. We enter Askrigg along a quiet lane leading to St Oswald's Church. The church was founded in 1125. On the SW exterior wall there is a tombstone of 'an honest attorney'.

Askrigg is an elegant village. It has a narrow main street lined with three-storey houses built during the seventeenth and eighteenth centuries. The village enjoyed a period of prosperity as a result of its many industries. These included clockmaking, cotton spinning, dyeing and hand-knitting. Askrigg became world-famous as Darrowby in the popular BBC series *All Creatures Great and Small.* Skeldale House, the vet's home in the series, is opposite the church.

Our route from Askrigg crosses the former Wensleydale railway line where a final causey leads us through the meadows to Worton. In 1757, due to the high price of corn, this peaceful hamlet became the scene of a bread riot. A quantity of corn, destined for some gentlemen from Upper Wharfedale, was stolen by an angry mob. The mob also demanded money from people in the surrounding villages. The offenders were eventually caught and imprisoned in Richmond Jail.

Leaving Worton we climb gently to the woodland of Thornton Scar where you may be lucky enough catch sight of a roe deer, as these shy little creatures take shelter in the wood. Another short climb through the wood returns us to the road at Thornton Rust.

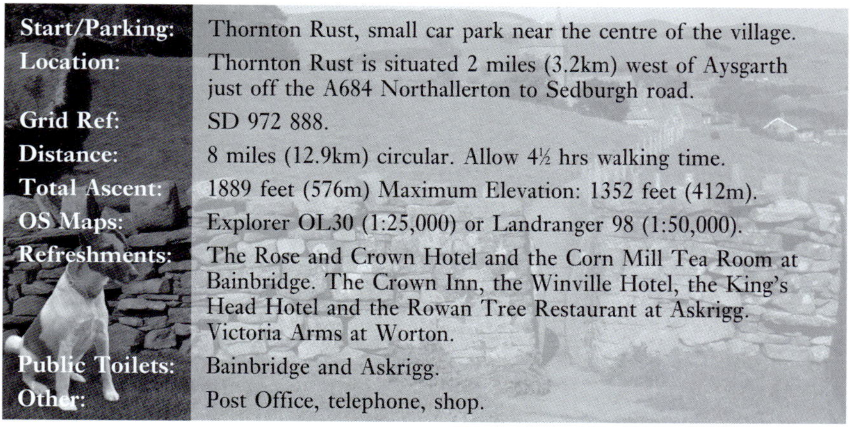

| | |
|---|---|
| **Start/Parking:** | Thornton Rust, small car park near the centre of the village. |
| **Location:** | Thornton Rust is situated 2 miles (3.2km) west of Aysgarth just off the A684 Northallerton to Sedburgh road. |
| **Grid Ref:** | SD 972 888. |
| **Distance:** | 8 miles (12.9km) circular. Allow 4½ hrs walking time. |
| **Total Ascent:** | 1889 feet (576m) Maximum Elevation: 1352 feet (412m). |
| **OS Maps:** | Explorer OL30 (1:25,000) or Landranger 98 (1:50,000). |
| **Refreshments:** | The Rose and Crown Hotel and the Corn Mill Tea Room at Bainbridge. The Crown Inn, the Winville Hotel, the King's Head Hotel and the Rowan Tree Restaurant at Askrigg. Victoria Arms at Worton. |
| **Public Toilets:** | Bainbridge and Askrigg. |
| **Other:** | Post Office, telephone, shop. |

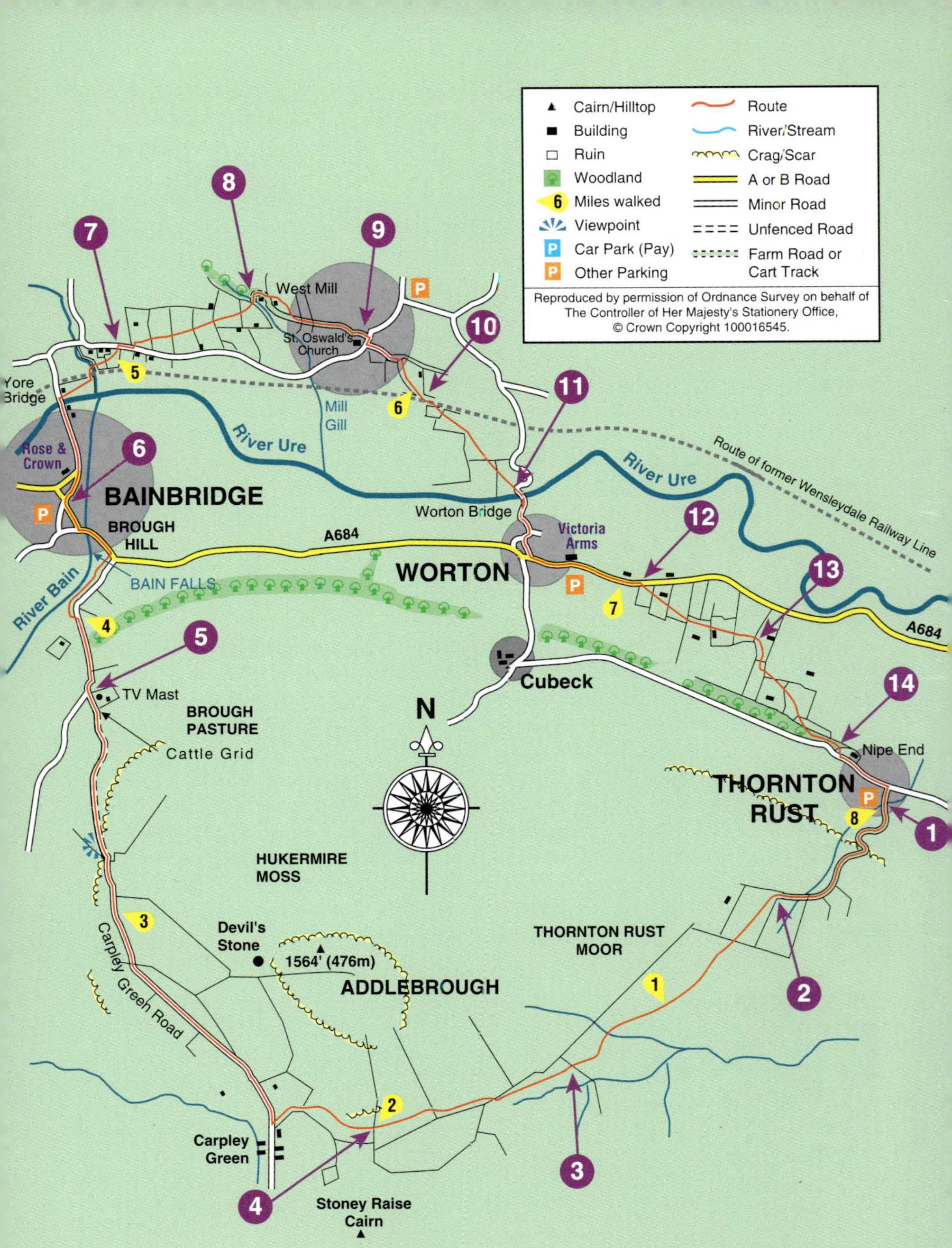


## THE DEVIL'S STONE

The large boulder visible just below the summit of Addlebrough is known as the Devil's Stone. According to local folklore the Devil threw this stone from Crag Hill near Semer Water at a giant on Addlebrough. The giant threw another stone at the Devil. This can be seen on the shore at Semer Water and is known as the Carlow Stone.

# Addlebrough and the Causeys

**1** *(GR 972 888)* From the car park follow the lane across a ford. Continue on a walled track which meanders uphill to a gate. Go through the gate, cross a stream and follow the track to the wall corner.

**2** *(GR 967 884)* At the wall corner bear left onto a clear track *(SP Bridleway)*. The track climbs up to a gate leading onto the open moor. Go through the gate and bear right slightly keeping roughly on the same heading to a ladder-stile.

**3** *(GR 958 876)* Cross the ladder-stile and continue ahead, gradually getting closer to the right wall. Go through a gate, turn left and follow the wall through two pastures to reach another gate.

**4** *(GR 948 873)* Go through the gate and continue over the shoulder of Addlebrough. Bear right and then descend left to go through a gate in the wall corner. Turn left and follow the wall down. Continue via a gate leading onto the road at Carpley Green. Turn right and follow the road downhill, passing a TV mast, to a T-junction.

**5** *(GR 935 893)* Turn right and continue descending along the road. After ¼ mile (360m) leave the road via a gap-stile on the left *(SP)*. Turn right and follow the wall down to another gap-stile leading onto the main road. Turn left and follow the road over the bridge and through Bainbridge passing the village stocks.

**6** *(GR 934 902)* Turn right onto the Askrigg road and follow it past the Rose and Crown Hotel. After crossing the river Ure *(Yorebridge)* go through a stile on the right *(SP Askrigg 1)*. Continue diagonally across the field joining a flagged path halfway. At a footbridge by the beck, turn left and cross a stone bridge further upstream. Go through two gates where another flagged path leads through two fields back to the main road.

**7** *(GR 936 910)* Turn right and after about 75 yards (70m) go through a stile on the left *(SP Footpath)* continue diagonally through 6 fields to Mill Gill.

**8** *(GR 943 912)* Cross the gill over a footbridge and follow a clear path to West Mill. Go through a gap-stile *(SP Askrigg)* and join a flagged path which leads onto a farm lane. Turn left and follow the lane past Askrigg Church to the main road.

**9** *(GR 948 910)* Leave Askrigg on the lane opposite the church between Skeldale House and Sykes House *(SP Worton/Aysgarth)*. When the surface of the lane becomes rougher fork right. Continue along a gravel path and go through a gate/stile. From the stile, continue close to the wall to the dismantled Wensleydale Railway line.

**10** *(GR 951 908)* Bear left and down some steps by a metal kissing-gate. Turn left on the track. After 30 yards (27m) leave the track near another kissing-gate on the right. Continue down through two gap-stiles onto a flagged causeway, follow this across three fields to the road at Worton Bridge.

**11** *(GR 955 903)* Turn right and cross the bridge. Continue up a steep hill and take the second turning on the left. At the main road turn left and follow the road through Worton passing the Victoria Arms.

**12** *(GR 961 899)* About ¼ mile (400m) past the Victoria Arms leave the road through a gap-stile on the right *(SP Thornton Rust 1)*. Follow a waymarked path diagonally across three fields. Cross a small stream and a wooden step-stile, then stay on a level course through three gap-stiles.

**13** *(GR 966 896)* Turn right following the fence uphill and go through a gap-stile. Bear left *(SP Footpath)* and go through two gap-stiles, cross a rutted track and climb over a small hill to a wooden step-stile. Cross the stile and climb up to a gap-stile, bear left and go through a gap-stile into the wood *(Thornton Scar)*. Turn left and after a few yards climb some steps. Continue on a clear path through the wood, to a gated stile *(Nipe End)*.

**14** *(GR 970 890)* Go through the stile and continue across the field to a gate leading onto the road at Thornton Rust. Turn left and follow the road to the village centre. At the village institute turn right returning to the car park.

(MAY 16) LOVELY WALK ABBEY NICE PUB AT COVER BRIDGE RENOWNED FOR HAM & EGGS! TRY NEXT TIME.

# 5

# JERVAULX ABBEY and THORNTON STEWARD

## FROM JERVAULX ABBEY 7½ MILES (12KM)

**This pleasant walk begins with a gentle stroll through the verdant parkland of Jervaulx. The terrain is almost level throughout and our return follows a peaceful riverside path.**

Jervaulx Abbey was founded in 1156 by Cistercian monks from Fors Abbey near Askrigg. The site at Fors was exposed to wind, rain and fog, making it unsuitable for crop production. This forced the monks to look for a more hospitable site. Jervaulx, with its rich pastures and sheltered position, proved to be the ideal choice. The abbey flourished for nearly 400 years and owned half of the land in Wensleydale. Jervaulx's prosperity came from sheep farming, horse breeding and cheese-making. The Jervaulx monks are credited as the original producers of Wensleydale cheese, but their exact recipe using ewes' milk has remained a secret.

Adam Sedbar, Jervaulx's last abbot, was involved in the famous protest against the dissolution – the ill-fated Pilgrimage of Grace. The King had already issued orders to find the ringleaders, the abbot was arrested, found guilty of high treason and hanged, drawn and quartered at Tyburn in 1537. In retribution for the abbot's sedition, Thomas Cromwell gave orders for the thorough demolition of Jervaulx. Today, little of the abbey church, which measured 270 feet (82m) by 63 feet (19m), is visible, but the ruins are still quite impressive.

After visiting the abbey we follow a quite farm lane through Jervaulx Park to Kilgram Bridge.

Kilgram Bridge is one of the oldest road bridges in Yorkshire dating back to at least 1540. Some authorities believe that the bridge was built by the monks of Jervaulx

Abbey in the twelfth century. The bridge's foundations are provided by a paved Roman ford. According to legend, the bridge was built by the Devil in return for the life of the first living creature to cross it. A local shepherd, knowing of this requirement, sent his obedient dog over the bridge first and the Devil's demand was satisfied. The dog's name was Grim and hence the bridge came to be known as Kil Grim Bridge and then Kilgram.

Our walk continues through flower-rich hay meadows to the sedate little hamlet of Thornton Steward. The village occupies a prominent position above the river Ure with wonderful views of Witton Fell. During the Napoleonic Wars, 1803-1815, a small corps of volunteers was stationed at Thornton Steward. At the eastern end of the village is a castellated square tower which they used as an armoury and store-room. Located half a mile to the west of the village is the interesting little church of St Oswald. Founded in the eleventh century, the church has a mixture of Anglo-Saxon, Norman and medieval architecture. Inside, there are fragments of some ninth-century crosses and an impressive sepulchral arch.

From the church we follow a good track passing Danby Hall. The hall, built in the early fourteenth century, was the former home of the powerful Scrope family. The Scrope's played a great part in English history. In 1378 Richard le Scrope became chancellor to Richard II. In 1398 another Richard le Scrope became Archbishop of York. He was convicted of conspiracy against Henry IV and executed in 1405. The Scrope family were also the founders of the beautiful little church of St Simon and St Jude near Ulshaw Bridge which was built in 1868.

Ulshaw Bridge is an impressive stone structure with four arches and three pairs of strong cutwaters. It is one of the most picturesque bridges across the Ure. The date it was built, 1674, is recorded on a sundial at the centre of the bridge.

Further along the road we arrive at the Cover Bridge Inn, where good food and a warm welcome are assured.

After crossing Cover Bridge, we join a riverside path which is followed to where the rivers Ure and Cover merge. They flow together almost unnoticeably, hidden by three wooded islands known as The Batts. The river at this point is said to be haunted by the Kelpie or Waterhorse! At certain times in the year, the Kelpie rises like a white mist from the water, rushing over the fields in an attempt to frighten his victims into the river.

We continue along the riverside to the boundary of Jervaulx Hall. Here a water level gauge indicates 310 feet (94m) above sea level. Raised embankments have been built to prevent flooding.

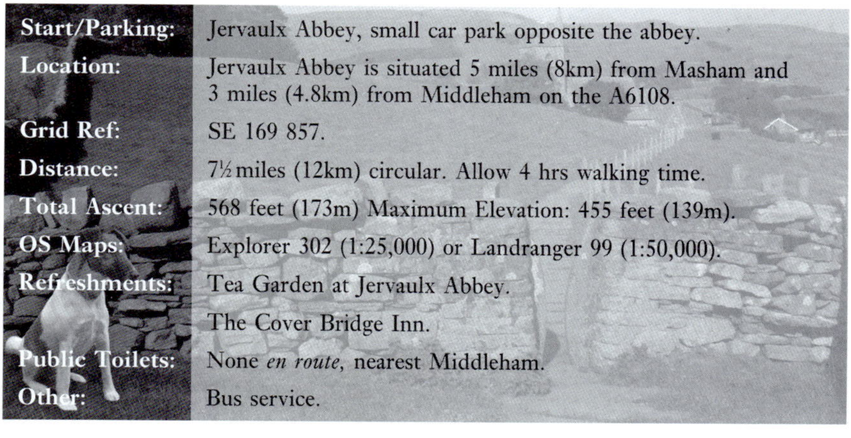

| | |
|---|---|
| **Start/Parking:** | Jervaulx Abbey, small car park opposite the abbey. |
| **Location:** | Jervaulx Abbey is situated 5 miles (8km) from Masham and 3 miles (4.8km) from Middleham on the A6108. |
| **Grid Ref:** | SE 169 857. |
| **Distance:** | 7½ miles (12km) circular. Allow 4 hrs walking time. |
| **Total Ascent:** | 568 feet (173m) Maximum Elevation: 455 feet (139m). |
| **OS Maps:** | Explorer 302 (1:25,000) or Landranger 99 (1:50,000). |
| **Refreshments:** | Tea Garden at Jervaulx Abbey. |
| | The Cover Bridge Inn. |
| **Public Toilets:** | None *en route*, nearest Middleham. |
| **Other:** | Bus service. |

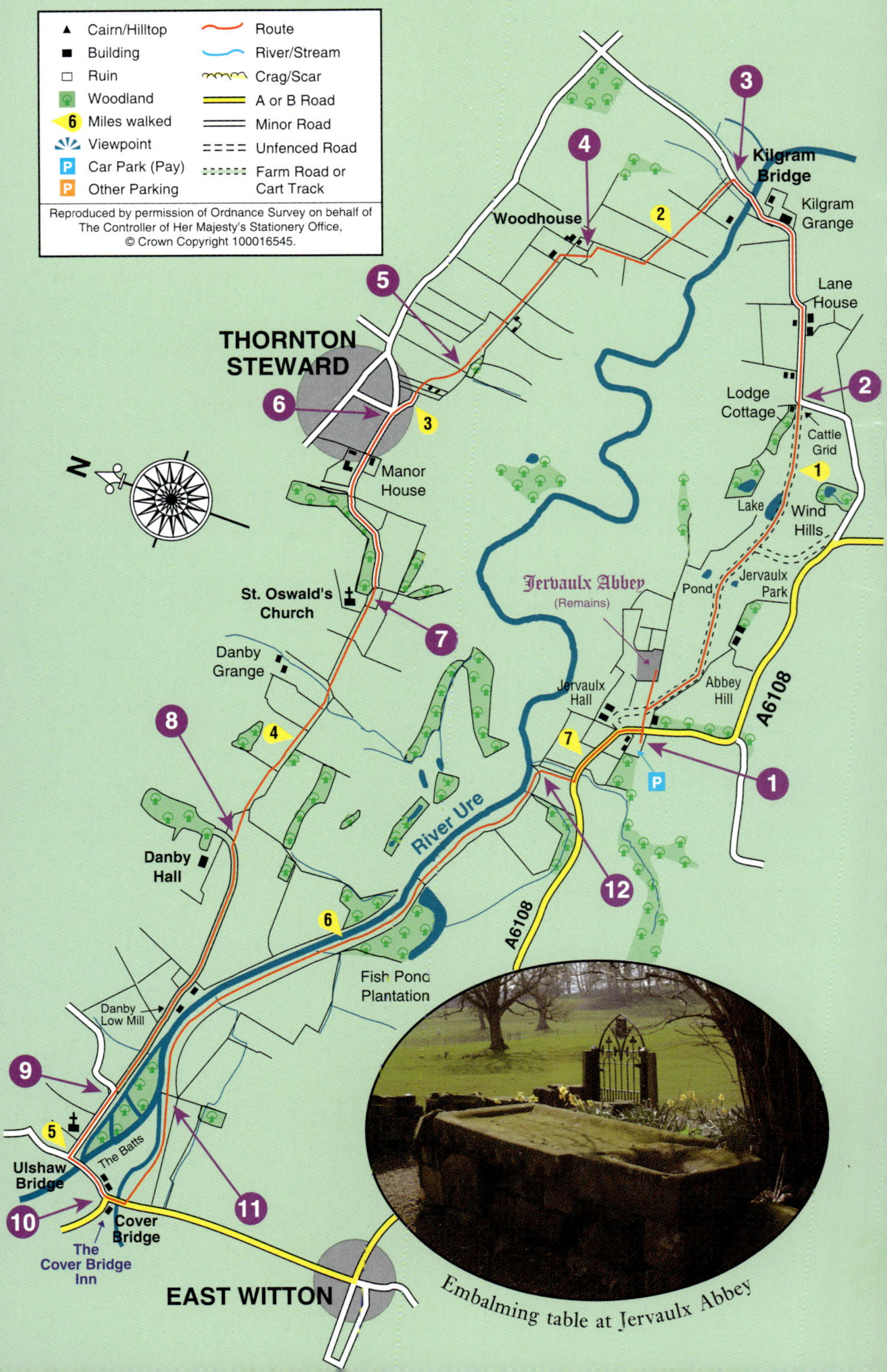


Embalming table at Jervaulx Abbey

# JERVAULX ABBEY AND THORNTON STEWARD

**1** *(GR 169 857)* From the car park cross the road and go through the gate opposite. Follow a narrow path which crosses a farm lane to the ruins of Jervaulx Abbey. After visiting the abbey return to the farm lane, turn left and follow the lane through Jervaulx Park. Continue through a gate beside a cattle grid to Lodge Cottage.

**2** *(GR 184 855)* Turn left onto the road and follow it to Kilgram Bridge. Cross the bridge and continue to the second pair of double gates on the left.

**3** *(GR 192 861)* Leave the road over a step-stile by the second pair of gates *(SP Public Footpath)*, continue straight ahead and go over another step-stile. Cross the next field to a stile with a waymark post. Follow the right hedge through the field and turn right. Continue through two gates to reach Woodhouse farm.

**4** *(GR 187 866)* Bear left and head towards the barn at the top left. Go through a gate, turn left and continue with the left hedge through three fields.

**5** *(GR 181 869)* Bear right to a gated stile marked with a white post. Continue across two narrow fields and go through a gate onto an enclosed track. Follow the track which leads into Thornton Steward.

**6** *(GR 178 871)* Turn left and follow the road through the village passing the old village water pump to a gate *(sign Manor House/St Oswald's Church only)*. Continue through the gate. When the lane forks, keep to the left walking downhill through two more gates to the small car park at St Oswald's Church.

**7** *(GR 170 869)* Go through a wooden gate, cross a cart track and follow the right boundary through two gates. Now continue with the left boundary through four more gates to reach Danby Hall.

**8** *(GR 160 871)* Turn left near the hall's entrance onto a farm lane which leads through some parkland. Go through two gates to reach the road.

**9** *(GR 149 872)* Turn left and continue along the road to the junction near the church of St Simon and St Jude. Turn left *(SP East Witton ¾)* and cross Ulshaw Bridge, follow the road to the Cover Bridge Inn.

**10** *(GR 144 871)* Turn left and cross the bridge over the river Cover. Leave the road almost immediately through a gate on the left *(SP Public Footpath)* and follow a riverside path to where the rivers of the Cover and Ure meet *(The Batts)*.

**11** *(GR 149 870)* Follow a riverside path through two gates to a fence which marks the boundary of Jervaulx Hall.

**12** *(GR 166 860)* Go through the gate on the right and follow the track to the main road. Turn left and follow the road back to the car park.

## THE CISTERCIANS - SAINTS OR SINNERS?

The Cistercians are usually thought of as an austere order who built their monasteries in wild and inhospitable places, where they lived a hard life, devoted to prayer and spirituality. However, when the earthwork remains at Jervaulx Abbey were surveyed in 1999 their reputation proved to be less virtuous. The survey revealed evidence that the monks evicted the local population when they founded their new abbey at Jervaulx. This ruthless act was not uncommon, abbeys had to be built in unpopulated areas to avoid corruption from the outside world and this resulted in many medieval villages being destroyed by the Cistercian Order. At least twenty villages are known to have suffered depopulation on the Fountains Abbey estates near Ripon.

(APRIL 16) NICE ONE NOT TOO DIFFICULT AT ALL.

# 6

# LEYBURN SHAWL and WENSLEY

## FROM LEYBURN 6 MILES (9.6KM)

**Wensleydale is overflowing with beautiful scenery and here is an opportunity to enjoy it with a minimum of effort. After an easy stroll along Leyburn Shawl, we pass through the parkland of Bolton Hall to Wensley and return via lush meadows to Leyburn.**

Leyburn, whose name means 'the stream by the clearing,' is a busy market town occupying a pleasant hilltop position above the northern bank of the river Ure. The market, granted its charter in 1684 by Charles II, is held every Friday when the large cobbled square is filled with vans and stalls. The arrival of the railway in 1856 helped to establish Leyburn as the main centre for the dale.

Frances I'Anson, the 'Sweet Lass of Richmond Hill', lived in Leyburn. The house where she was born is situated in the High Street and is inscribed 'W.I.A. 1746' above the door. Her husband, Leonard McNally, wrote the well known song about her.

Our path from Leyburn follows a natural limestone terrace, known as the Shawl. It is a rocky scar, two miles long, commanding spectacular views across to Penhill, into Coverdale and along the broad valley of Wensleydale. In 1841 a promenade was laid out with seats and shelters, attracting many visitors of the highest respectability. Tea galas, music and dancing were supported by the Band of Hope who encouraged total abstinence. The Leyburn Shawl Tea Festival of 1844 was attended by more than 2,000 people.

According to local tradition, Mary, Queen of Scots dropped her shawl near here after escaping from Bolton Castle in 1568, and thus gave the Shawl its name. The lost shawl betrayed her whereabouts and she was recaptured at a spot known as the Queen's Gap. However, the Shawl more likely takes its name from 'shieling' which means a farm or summer pasture.

Leaving the scar, we descend to Tullis Cote passing close to the site of a Bronze Age settlement. Although little is visible today, remains of cave dwellings, bones, charcoal, grinding stones and flints have been found here.

The square chimney below Tullis Cote Farm belongs to the old pumping engine house of the Keld Head Mine, the largest leadmine in Wensleydale. At one time it employed 300 men from the surrounding villages. Until its closure in 1888, the mine produced 1,374 tons of smelted ore each year. The smelt mill was sited higher on the hill. It had a two mile flue to carry poisonous fumes up the hillside and away from the valley. When the Wensleydale railway line first opened, it was a standard joke to tell the passengers to watch out for the two mile long chimney, which they would have expected to see rising high into the sky.

After crossing the railway line our route continues through the lush parkland of the Bolton Hall estate to Wensley. The Hall was built in 1678 by the eccentric Charles Powlett, Marquis of Winchester, who became the first Duke of Bolton. One of his odd pastimes was hunting at night by the light of torches. It is also said that he would not speak during the day until he thought the air was pure. The hall contains many fine paintings including several by Van Dyck, the Flemish painter.

Wensley is a peaceful and unspoiled village from which the Dale takes its name. It was Wensleydale's first market town, receiving its charter in 1202. The village flourished until the plague of 1563, when many of the surviving population fled to Leyburn. Wensley never recovered from the effects of this pestilence and lost its status as a market town.

The parish church is outstanding and bears witness to Wensley's former status. It dates from 1245, although a number of renovations have been carried out since that time. The sanctuary has a fourteenth-century Flemish memorial brass to the priest, Sir Simon de Wenselawe. The finely carved oak screen surrounding the Bolton family pews was brought from Easby Abbey after the dissolution. The churchyard contains the grave of Peter Goldsmith, the surgeon aboard *HMS Victory*, in whose arms Lord Nelson died at Trafalgar.

Our return to Leyburn passes Leyburn Old Glebe, a traditional dales' meadow and a haven for a wide variety of wild flowers, including the green-winged and burnt tip orchids. At Low Wood Lane a narrow flowery lane leads us back to the market place.

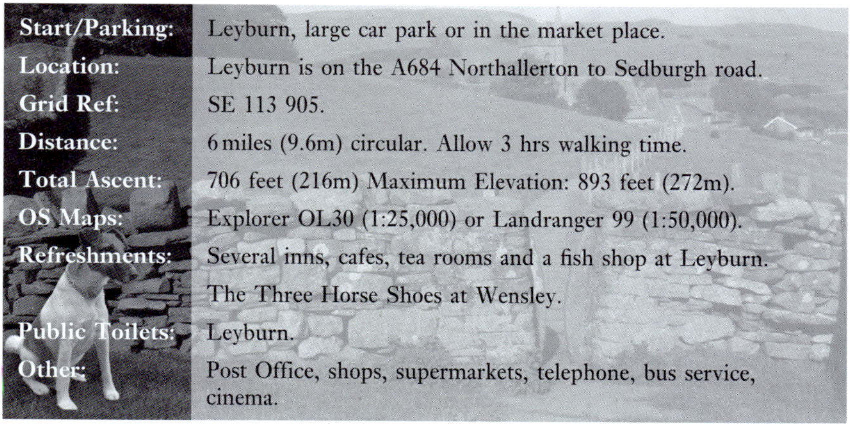

| | |
|---|---|
| **Start/Parking:** | Leyburn, large car park or in the market place. |
| **Location:** | Leyburn is on the A684 Northallerton to Sedburgh road. |
| **Grid Ref:** | SE 113 905. |
| **Distance:** | 6 miles (9.6m) circular. Allow 3 hrs walking time. |
| **Total Ascent:** | 706 feet (216m) Maximum Elevation: 893 feet (272m). |
| **OS Maps:** | Explorer OL30 (1:25,000) or Landranger 99 (1:50,000). |
| **Refreshments:** | Several inns, cafes, tea rooms and a fish shop at Leyburn. The Three Horse Shoes at Wensley. |
| **Public Toilets:** | Leyburn. |
| **Other:** | Post Office, shops, supermarkets, telephone, bus service, cinema. |

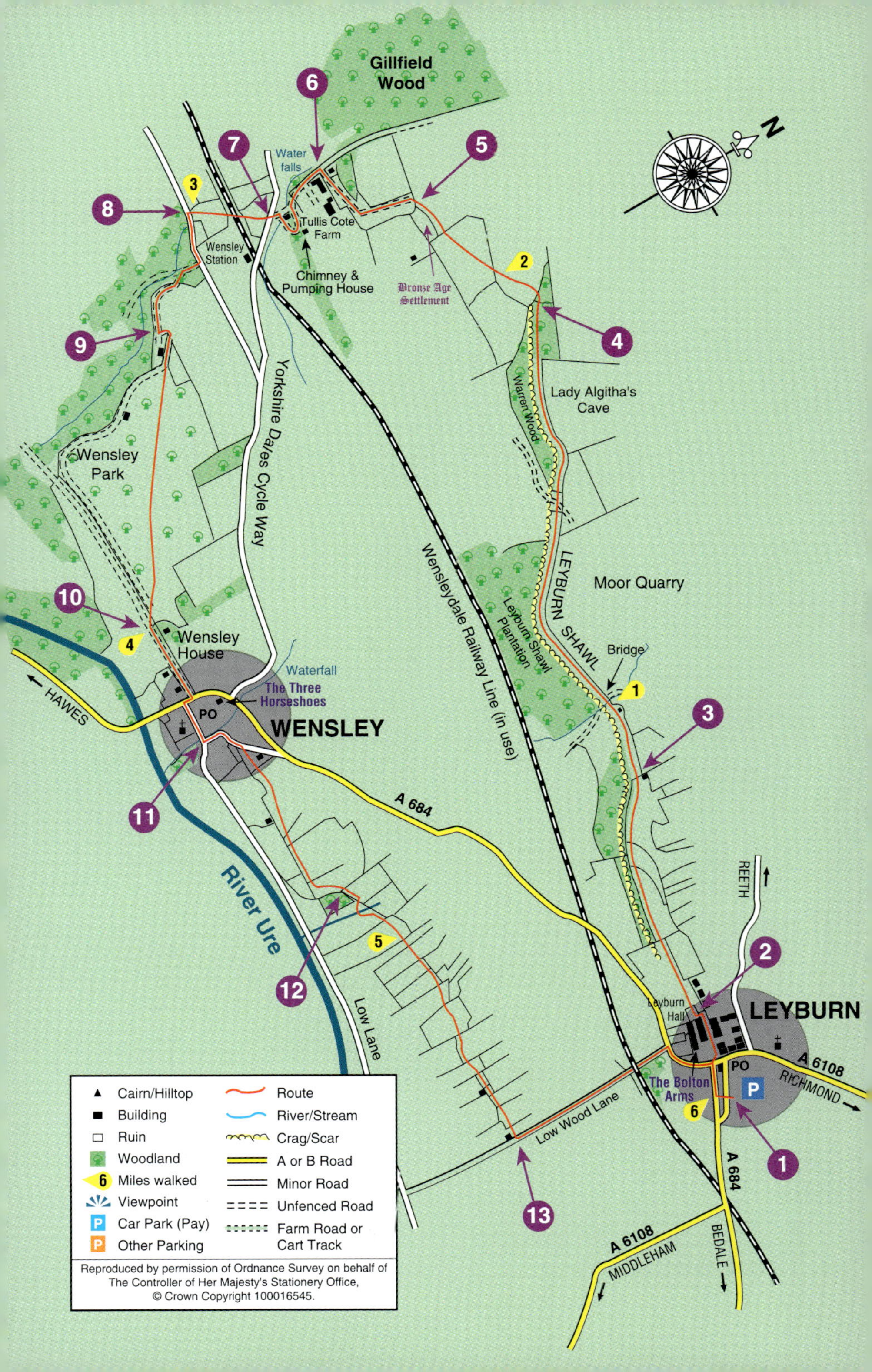
Gillfield Wood
Water falls
Tullis Cote Farm
Chimney & Pumping House
Bronze Age Settlement
Wensley Station
Wensley Park
Yorkshire Dales Cycle Way
Wensleydale Railway Line (in use)
Lady Algitha's Cave
Warren Wood
LEYBURN SHAWL
Moor Quarry
Leyburn Shawl Plantation
Bridge
Wensley House
Waterfall
The Three Horseshoes
PO
WENSLEY
HAWES
A 684
River Ure
Low Lane
Low Wood Lane
REETH
LEYBURN
Leyburn Hall
The Bolton Arms
A 6108
RICHMOND
MIDDLEHAM
BEDALE
N
1 2 3 4 5 6 7 8 9 10 11 12 13
Cairn/Hilltop
Building
Ruin
Woodland
Miles walked
Viewpoint
Car Park (Pay)
Other Parking
Route
River/Stream
Crag/Scar
A or B Road
Minor Road
Unfenced Road
Farm Road or Cart Track

# Leyburn Shawl and Wensley

**1** *(GR 113 905)* From the car park return to the market square and walk towards the Bolton Arms. Pass to the right of the inn and leave the square by the side of Campbell and Sons *(SP Way to the Shawl)*. Follow a short lane to another sign *(SP to the Shawl)* turn left and go through a gate onto a flagged path.

**2** *(GR 110 905)* Follow the flagged path through a gate and begin climbing gradually uphill passing through a gate and two stiles to reach a field with a barn in the far right corner.

**3** *(GR 102 908)* Go through the stile in the left corner and enter a woodland area. Cross a high bridge *(over the road to the quarry)* and follow a clear track along the top of the scar.

**4** *(GR 086 913)* Descend over two stiles to leave the wood. Continue descending and cross a stile to the right of a gate. Bear half right and go through a gate in the far side of the field. Follow the left fence round to a gate leading into a narrow field.

**5** *(GR 081 911)* Go through the gate and follow a farm track downhill. At a junction of tracks turn right, go through a gate and pass through the farmyard at Tullis Cote.

**6** *(GR 079 910)* Leave the farmyard, turn left and follow the lane through a gate, continue with the right wall and descend on a rougher track through another gate. Turn left and follow the track down past the chimney and former pumping engine house to the road.

**7** *(GR 079 907)* Cross the road and go through the gate opposite. Continue directly across the field. Cross the railway track via two stiles, cross the field and go through a gate leading onto the main road.

**8** *(GR 077 905)* Turn left and follow the road for about 200 yards (182m) then turn right onto a track leading into woodland *(SP Public Footpath)*. Follow this track for 25 yards (23m) and turn left to leave the wood via a gate beside a cattle grid. Follow the track along the right fence.

**9** *(GR 080 902)* At a gate turn left and follow the fence round to another gate. Go through the gate and follow a track to the left of a barn. When the track leads off to the right leave it. Continue in roughly the same direction across the parkland of Wensley Park and begin a gradual descent towards Wensley House.

**10** *(GR 089 896)* Go through a gate joining the concrete estate road. Turn left and follow the road over a cattle grid to the main A684 road. Turn right and cross the road. At the T-junction turn left *(Middleham, Masham, Ripon)*. Follow the road past the church and cross a bridge.

**11** *(GR 093 896)* After crossing the bridge turn left and pass in front of a white house onto a narrow road. Follow this road for approximately 150 yards (137m). At a left hand bend leave the road through a gate on the right *(SP Public Footpath)* and follow a waymarked path through a gate and three stiles. Bear left and climb up to a stile at the left side of the wood.

**12** *(GR 100 897)* Go through the stile, follow the right wall for about 25 yards (23m) and go through a stile on the right. Cross a plank bridge and return to the wall-side, keeping roughly to the same level. Follow a waymarked path through more than a dozen fields to finally emerge into Low Wood Lane.

**13** *(GR 110 898)* Turn left and climb this steep narrow lane passing under the railway line to return to the main A684 road. Turn right at the main road and follow it back to Leyburn market place.

(MAY 16) GOOD ONE BIT OF ROAD (QUIET) BUT MADE UP LATER WITH OPEN MOOR.

# 7

# MIDDLEHAM LOW MOOR and the RIVER COVER

## FROM MIDDLEHAM 7¾ MILES (12.5KM)

**This leisurely ramble explores the beautiful and peaceful valley of Coverdale. It visits the impressive ruins of Middleham Castle, once known as the Windsor of the North.**

Middleham is a small market town with two market squares, each having its own cross. It was granted its first charter in 1389. In the upper market square is the Swine Cross, so called because of a stone carving which crudely resembles a pig. This is believed to represent the white boar emblem of Richard, Duke of Gloucester who granted the market a second charter in 1479.

Middleham Castle, dating from 1170, boasts a keep which is second in size only to the Tower of London. It was built for residence rather than defence by Robert FitzRandolph. In 1270, ownership of the castle passed by marriage to the Neville family. The Nevilles were very powerful with the greatest of them all, Richard Neville, Earl of Warwick, known as 'the Kingmaker.' After Warwick's death at the battle of Barnet, the castle was given to Richard, Duke of Gloucester, who later became Richard III.

Richard arrived at Middleham in 1461 as a boy of eleven. Here he was educated and received his training to become a knight. He married Anne Neville, Warwick's daughter, whom he had loved since childhood. They lived happily at Middleham Castle until 1483, when King Edward IV died and Richard became protector to the new king, a boy of twelve. Richard seized the throne for himself, confining the young king and his brother to the Tower. Whether or not Richard murdered the princes has never been proved. However, his reign was short-lived as he was killed at the battle of Bosworth in 1485.

After leaving Middleham our route crosses Middleham Low Moor, where strings of racehorses are often seen on their way to the gallops. Middleham, the Newmarket of the North, is renowned for its blood-stock breeding, with a dozen or so trainers producing some of England's finest racehorses. There are superb views of two valleys; to the left Coverdale with Buckden Pike at its head and to the right Wensleydale with Penhill.

At Fern Gill we leave the moor and our path descends past the racing stables and some ornamental ponds to the road, which we follow to Coverham Bridge.

A short distance from the bridge are the remains of Coverham Abbey. The abbey was founded *c.*1202 for the White Canons of the Premonstratensian order. They had moved from their original site at Swainby in the Vale of Mowbray, most probably to be closer to their patrons who lived at Middleham Castle. The abbot's quarters and guesthouse were converted into a private house after the dissolution. The garden contains the remains of the south arcade of the abbey church. The abbey remains are in private grounds but the gatehouse can be seen from the road.

We continue across Coverham Bridge which has a steep single arch. Then a quiet lane leads us gently uphill to the hamlet of Caldbergh. Dr. Miles Coverdale, Bishop of Exeter, was born here in 1488. He translated the Bible into English from the German and Latin versions in 1535.

From Caldbergh our route passes below the site of an Iron Age hill fort known as Castle Steads. The fort was used by the Brigantes during their resistance to the Romans. On reaching Hanghow Pastures there are wonderful views across the valley to Middleham Low Moor and the racing stables of Ferngill, Tupgill and Thorngill, which we passed earlier in the walk. Coverham Abbey can also be seen in the valley bottom.

After descending to the road we pass Braithwaite Hall, a seventeenth-century manor house, now a working hill farm. The hall was built on the site of a former grange of Jervaulx Abbey. It is a National Trust property and can be visited by prior arrangement. From the hall we follow a broad track to Hullo Bridge where a single stone arch spans the rocky bed of the river Cover.

Our return to Middleham passes close to William's Hill, the site of Middleham's first motte and bailey castle. It consisted of a mound forty feet high within a ditch and bank, and had a wooden tower. There is a legend that anyone who runs three times round the hill – some say seven or nine - will discover an opening into the mound giving access to great treasure.

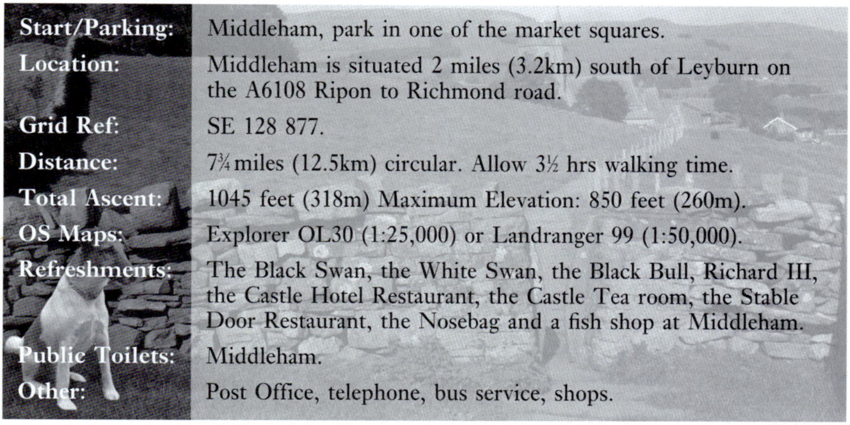

| | |
|---|---|
| **Start/Parking:** | Middleham, park in one of the market squares. |
| **Location:** | Middleham is situated 2 miles (3.2km) south of Leyburn on the A6108 Ripon to Richmond road. |
| **Grid Ref:** | SE 128 877. |
| **Distance:** | 7¾ miles (12.5km) circular. Allow 3½ hrs walking time. |
| **Total Ascent:** | 1045 feet (318m) Maximum Elevation: 850 feet (260m). |
| **OS Maps:** | Explorer OL30 (1:25,000) or Landranger 99 (1:50,000). |
| **Refreshments:** | The Black Swan, the White Swan, the Black Bull, Richard III, the Castle Hotel Restaurant, the Castle Tea room, the Stable Door Restaurant, the Nosebag and a fish shop at Middleham. |
| **Public Toilets:** | Middleham. |
| **Other:** | Post Office, telephone, bus service, shops. |

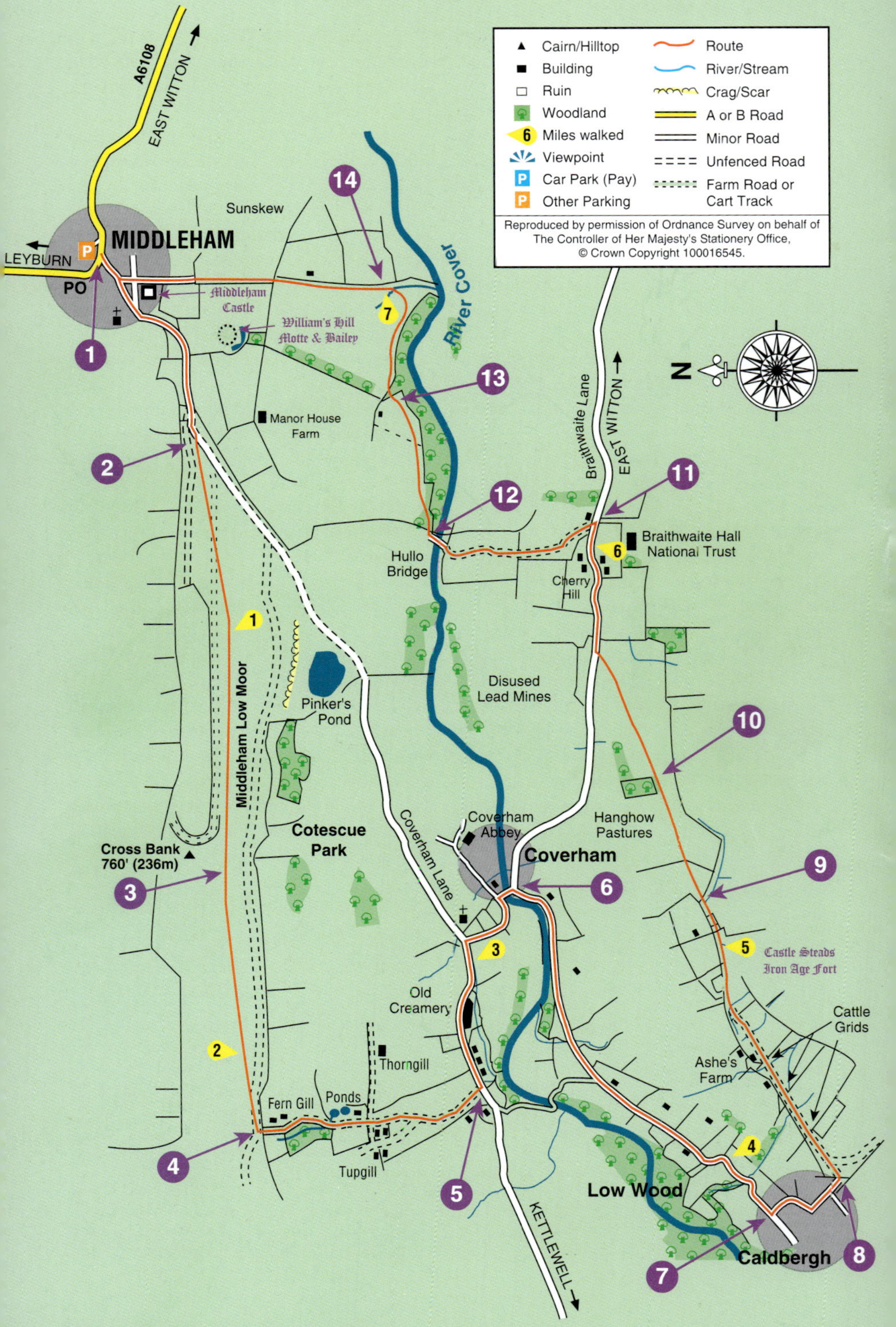

Cairn/Hilltop
Building
Ruin
Woodland
Miles walked
Viewpoint
Car Park (Pay)
Other Parking
Route
River/Stream
Crag/Scar
A or B Road
Minor Road
Unfenced Road
Farm Road or Cart Track
Reproduced by permission of Ordnance Survey on behalf of The Controller of Her Majesty's Stationery Office, © Crown Copyright 100016545.
A6108
EAST WITTON
LEYBURN
MIDDLEHAM
PO
Sunskew
Middleham Castle
William's Hill Motte & Bailey
Manor House Farm
River Cover
Braithwaite Lane
EAST WITTON
Braithwaite Hall National Trust
Cherry Hill
Hullo Bridge
Disused Lead Mines
Pinker's Pond
Middleham Low Moor
Cotescue Park
Cross Bank 760' (236m)
Coverham Abbey
Coverham
Hanghow Pastures
Coverham Lane
Castle Steads Iron Age Fort
Old Creamery
Thorngill
Cattle Grids
Ashe's Farm
Fern Gill
Ponds
Tupgill
Low Wood
Caldbergh
KETTLEWELL

# Middleham Low Moor and the River Cover

**1** *(GR 128 877)* Leave the market square and follow the Kettlewell/Carlton road out of Middleham, passing the Swine Cross and Jubilee Fountain.

**2** *(GR 122 874)* When the road reaches the moor go through a gate in the right fence *(SP Public Bridleway)* and begin a gentle ascent onto Middleham Low Moor. Cross a broad track. *(This is not a public right of way, it is an all-weather track used by the nearby horse racing stables).* Keep to the left of this track and follow it uphill. Pass to the left of a standing stone and continue towards the Ordnance Survey column at Cross Bank.

**3** *(GR 106 872)* Near the OS column bear left and begin to descend slightly. Continue in the same direction keeping in line with the left boundary wall. When the first buildings come into view behind the wall head towards them and join a broad, stone track.

**4** *(GR 095 871)* Go through the stone gateway on the left. Follow the gravel track down past two ornamental ponds and through a pair of gates to join a tarmac lane. Continue down the lane which leads to the main road.

**5** *(GR 097 863)* Turn left onto the road, go past some houses and an old creamery on the right. At the road junction turn right *(SP Caldbergh 1)*, continue along the road and cross over Coverham Bridge.

**If you wish to visit Coverham Church go through the lych-gate on the right just beyond the junction.**

**6** *(GR 104 862)* Turn right *(SP Caldbergh 1¼)* and follow a quiet lane which leads gently uphill to Caldbergh.

**7** *(GR 093 852)* Turn left *(SP Caldbergh only)* and continue climbing uphill through the village. Go past the telephone box to reach a gate.

**8** *(GR 094 850)* Go through the gate *(SP Braithwaite 1½)*. and follow a farm track over three cattle grids to reach Ashe's Farm. From the farm continue straight ahead on a rougher track. After going through a gate the track gradually peters out. Go through another gate and a sheep pen. Continue alongside the left wall to the next gate.

**9** *(GR 104 855)* Go through the gate, head straight across the field and go through a gate in the fence. The path continues through a large pasture *(Hanghow Pastures)* passing to the right of a small wood.

**10** *(GR 109 857)* From the wood continue through the pasture and begin a gradual descent to the far corner of the field. Go over a wooden stile leading onto the road. Turn right and follow the road to the entrance of Braithwaite Hall.

**11** *(GR 118 859)* Turn left opposite the entrance *(SP BW Hullo Bridge ⅓)*. Go through a gate, follow a clear track to the river Cover. Continue across Hullo Bridge.

**12** *(GR 118 865)* From the bridge go over a wooden stile on the right and join a clear track leading up through the trees. Turn right and follow the fence. After passing through a former hedgerow bear left and climb up towards the corner of a wood.

**13** *(GR 123 867)* Cross two wooden stiles leading through the wood, turn right and continue beside the fence. When the fence drops away, bear left, heading straight across the field and cross a small stream.

**14** *(GR 127 866)* Turn left at the boundary, follow the right fence through a gate and then follow the left wall through another gate leading onto a rough lane by the castle. At the end of the lane cross a road and continue down a ginnel between the houses. At the main road turn right and return to the market square.

# 8

# MOSSDALE and COTTERDALE

## FROM APPERSETT 7¾ MILES (12.5KM)

**Starting from the sleepy village of Appersett, this walk visits two secluded valleys at the head of Wensleydale. Apart from a few steep climbs the walking is fairly easy and the views are absolutely superb.**

Mossdale is Wensleydale's smallest side valley, stretching from Appersett to the Mossdale viaduct. Appersett, lying in a sheltered position below the slopes of Widdale Fell, is a peaceful village with most of its cottages facing away from the main road. The green, enclosed between the road and Widdale Beck, was once overcrowded with ducks, geese, goats and children, but nowadays it serves mainly as a car park. Appersett, like many of the villages in the upper dale, is of Norse origin and the name means 'The shieling near the apple tree' – a 'shieling' was a farm or summer pasture.

Leaving Appersett we follow the road over Widdale Beck to New Bridge, where we descend to the bank of the river Ure. Our path continues through pastures, woodland and meadows to the farm road near Birk Rigg Farm.

From here, a detour to visit the most attractive waterfall of Cotter Force is highly recommended. A short and easy stroll along the tree-lined Cotterdale Beck leads us to the secluded waterfall, which cascades over a series of limestone ledges on its way to join the river Ure further downstream.

After returning from the falls, our route leads back to the river and then continues to Mossdale Head. The four-arched viaduct, crossing the ravine of Mossdale Beck, once carried a branch line of the Wensleydale Railway from Garsdale Head to Hawes. This route linked to the Settle and Carlisle line. The branch line was almost six miles in length. Climbing steadily from Hawes it attained a height of over 1000 feet (305m) at Garsdale Head. This new section of line, passing through beautiful but very rugged countryside, required the construction of several viaducts and a 245 yard (224m) tunnel near Mossdale Head. The views, after emerging from the gloomy tunnel, must have been inspiring.

The area around here is much quieter now and the silence is broken only by the cascading waterfalls of Mossdale Beck. The beck rises on Widdale Fell, whose summit stands at 2203 feet (672m) and is called Great Knoutberry Hill. The upper falls, painted by J. M. W. Turner during his tour of 1816-18, are about a quarter of a mile further upstream. Turner had been commissioned to make 120 watercolours which were to be used as illustrations in a grand, seven-volume *General History of the County of York* by Longmans. A Turner seat, near Mossdale House Farm, allows visitors to rest and enjoy a view of the lower falls, which are framed by one of the viaduct's arches.

Our route continues to Thwaite Bridge where we follow a steep track over the ridge of Cotter End and into Cotterdale. As we begin our descent some of the most spectacular views of the walk are to be seen. Lunds Fell to the west and Great Shunner Fell to the east rise up from this peaceful and secluded side valley.

Cotterdale, 'the valley with the huts,' is also the name taken by the sedate little hamlet at the head of the valley. Being situated at the end of a narrow lane, it became the subject of a rhyme when three of its families were the Halls, Kirks and Kings;

*Three Halls, two Kirks and a King,*
*Same road out as goes in.*

A survey, taken in 1603, shows that six titled or wealthy men occupied houses in the hamlet. They were descendants of men involved in Catholic plots in the reign of Elizabeth I, and their ancestors are likely to have been given the houses for refuge during times of persecution. There is also evidence of an Iron Age settlement in Cotterdale, a sword dating around AD 50 was found here and is now in the British Museum.

Leaving the village our path traverses the lower slopes of Great Shunner Fell, with exceptional views of Cotterdale and Wensleydale. To the south Wether Fell, Dodd Fell and Widdale Fell dominate the landscape. Cotter End lies to the west and winding its way through the valley bottom is Cotterdale Beck.

After crossing Bluebell Hill, we follow a section of the Pennine Way before descending through the fields to the road which we follow back to Appersett.

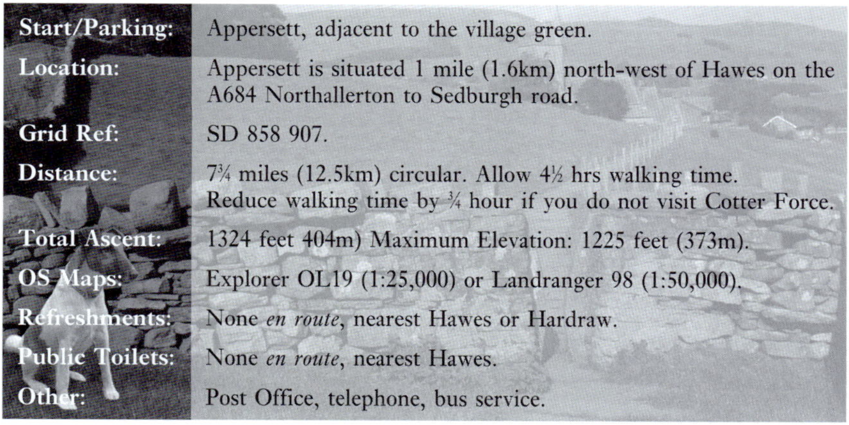

| | |
|---|---|
| **Start/Parking:** | Appersett, adjacent to the village green. |
| **Location:** | Appersett is situated 1 mile (1.6km) north-west of Hawes on the A684 Northallerton to Sedburgh road. |
| **Grid Ref:** | SD 858 907. |
| **Distance:** | 7¾ miles (12.5km) circular. Allow 4½ hrs walking time. Reduce walking time by ¾ hour if you do not visit Cotter Force. |
| **Total Ascent:** | 1324 feet 404m) Maximum Elevation: 1225 feet (373m). |
| **OS Maps:** | Explorer OL19 (1:25,000) or Landranger 98 (1:50,000). |
| **Refreshments:** | None *en route*, nearest Hawes or Hardraw. |
| **Public Toilets:** | None *en route*, nearest Hawes. |
| **Other:** | Post Office, telephone, bus service. |

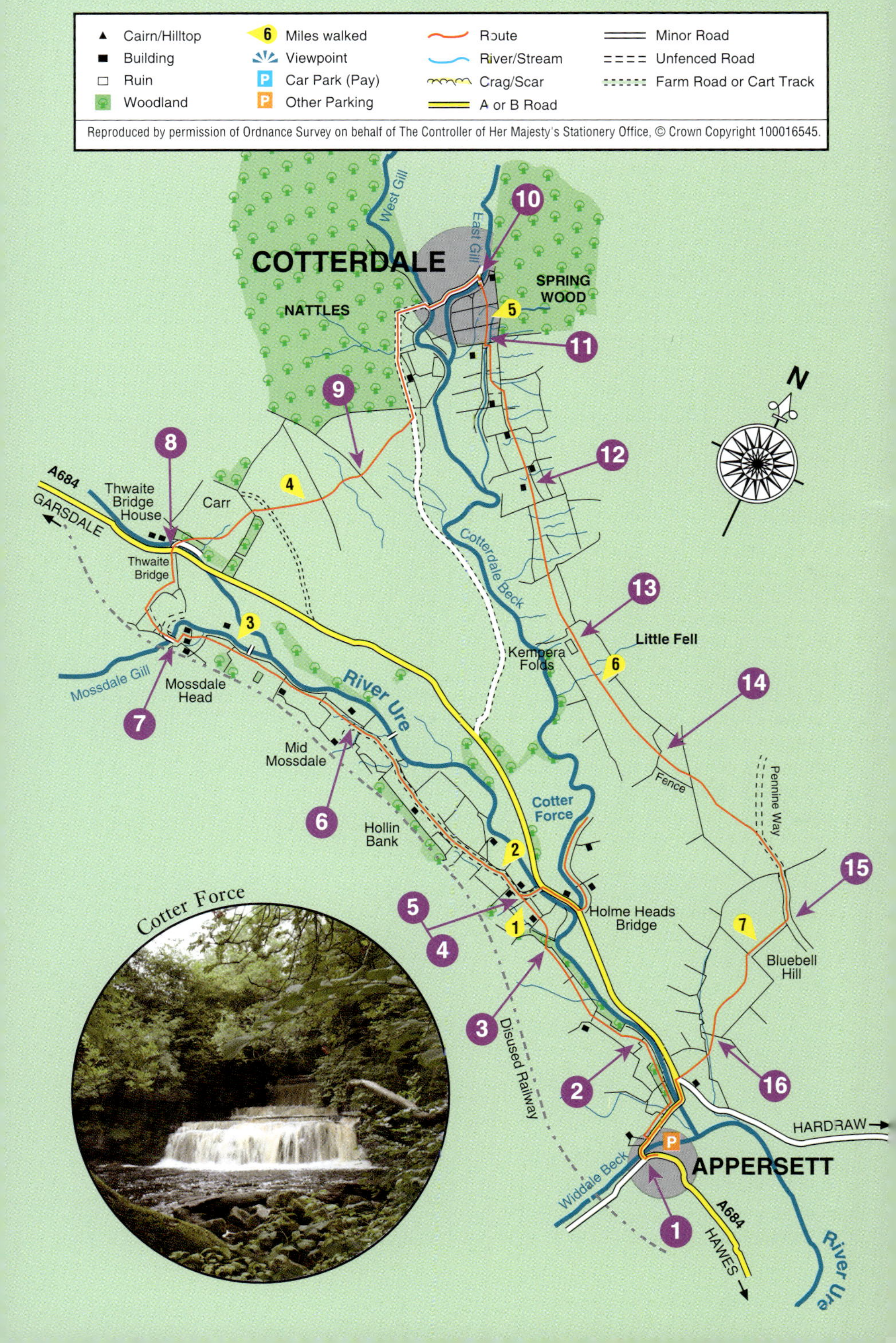

Cairn/Hilltop
Building
Ruin
Woodland
Miles walked
Viewpoint
Car Park (Pay)
Other Parking
Route
River/Stream
Crag/Scar
A or B Road
Minor Road
Unfenced Road
Farm Road or Cart Track
COTTERDALE
NATTLES
SPRING WOOD
West Gill
East Gill
N
A684
GARSDALE
Thwaite Bridge House
Carr
Thwaite Bridge
Mossdale Gill
Mossdale Head
River Ure
Mid Mossdale
Hollin Bank
Cotterdale Beck
Kempera Folds
Little Fell
Fence
Pennine Way
Cotter Force
Holme Heads Bridge
Bluebell Hill
Disused Railway
HARDRAW
APPERSETT
Widdale Beck
HAWES
Cotter Force
1
2
3
4
5
6
7
8
9
10
11
12
13
14
15
16

# Mossdale and Cotterdale

**1** *(GR 858 907)* Cross the bridge over Widdale Beck and go through a stile on the left *(SP Mossdale Head 2m)*. Follow the wall through two stiles to the river Ure at New Bridge. Continue upstream via a step-stile and pass through a small wood to a ladder-stile.

**2** *(GR 855 912)* Cross the stile, bear left to leave the riverbank, climbing up to pass along the top of a wood. Go over another ladder-stile *(SP Mossdale Head)*. Bear right across a large depression and follow the right wall through a gap-stile to a ladder-stile.

**3** *(GR 850 913)* Go over the ladder-stile and descend through the wood on a clear path. Cross a small beck, bear left and continue through a gate to the right of a barn. Follow the right wall through a gate *(SP Mossdale Head)* onto a farm road.

**4** *(GR 847 915)* To visit Cotter Force turn right *(SP A684)* and at the main road turn right. After crossing Holme Heads Bridge leave the road *(SP Cotter Force ¼)*. Go through a gate on the left and follow a clear path to the falls. Return to point 5.

**5** *(GR 847 915)* Follow the farm road through two gates and then fork left onto another track. Stay on this track through four more gates.

**6** *(GR 937 918)* Leave the track staying with the right wall through a gate and then follow the river upstream through three more gates to Mossdale Head Farm. Pass just to the right of the farmhouse and around the barn to reach a bridge.

**7** *(GR 827 919)* Cross the bridge and continue straight ahead through two gates. Bear right and follow the line of a derelict wall uphill. Go through a gate, turn right and follow the wall round. Descend to the road at Thwaite Bridge House.

**8** *(GR 826 922)* Cross the road and then Thwaite Bridge *(SP Cotterdale 1)*. Follow a clear path through the wood *(SP Cotterdale Rd 1)* climbing gradually, to a ladder-stile. Cross the stile, bear right and climb through the steep pasture to a ladder-stile in the top right hand corner. Continue in the same direction over two more stiles.

**9** *(GR 832 929)* Bear left and descend along a clear path to reach the Cotterdale road near a cattle grid. Turn left and follow this quiet road over the cattle grid into the hamlet of Cotterdale.

**10** *(GR 833 940)* Almost at the end of the hamlet leave the road over a footbridge on the right *(SP Hardraw 3)*. Go through a gate and cross two fields via two stiles. Continue below a small stream to a gated stile.

**11** *(GR 835 937)* Go through the stile and follow the fenced stream along the bottom of the field. Go through a gap in a broken wall and bear left, climbing up to a stile in the top wall. Turn right and follow the right wall through a broken wall. Continue via a stile above a barn and go through a gate below the next barn.

**12** *(GR 839 933)* Pass above the barn and climb up through a stile. Continue along a clear path through the bracken passing through a stile and a gate to arrive at an old sheepfold *(Kempera Folds)*.

**13** *(GR 844 927)* Continue through a large pasture, keeping roughly to the same level. Approaching the next wall climb up to go through a derelict waymarked stile.

**14** *(GR 850 924)* Pass to the right of a short section of wall, and descend to a ladder-stile bearing slightly to the left. From the stile head straight across the moor to arrive at a wide track *(The Pennine Way)*. Turn right and descend through a gate/ladder-stile onto a walled lane.

**15** *(GR 859 919)* Leave the lane at the first gate on the right *(SP New Bridge ⅜)*, follow the left wall descending steeply to cross a ladder-stile. Continue descending through a large pasture and go through a gate in the bottom left of the field.

**16** *(GR 858 913)* Bear right and descend to go through a gate, cross the field to a gap-stile leading onto the road. Follow the A684 Hawes road back to Appersett.

# FORELANDS RIGG and WALDEN BECK

## FROM WEST BURTON 8¼ MILES (10.1KM)

**This spectacular walk visits the side valleys of Bishopdale and Walden. Separated by the Wasset Fell ridge, they provide a rich contrast of landscapes and offer many opportunities for birdwatchers and botanists.**

West Burton stands at the entrance to the secret valley of Walden. It boasts an enormous green extending almost the full length of the village. The market cross was erected in 1820 and is most unusual, being more like a church spire resting on a flight of steps. Adjacent to the cross are the stocks which were certainly in use in 1660 when a quaker, Samuel Watson of Knight Stainforth, attempted to hold a religious meeting here against the wishes of the villagers. For expressing his beliefs he was dragged down by the crowd, severely beaten, ridiculed in the stocks and then thrown into the river.

At one time residents of West Burton found guilty of wife beating or adultery had to undergo a form of public ridicule known as 'Riding the Stang.' The 'stang' was a stout piece of wood to which the guilty person was tied. They were then carried round the village, closely pursued by a crowd of shouting, whistling and screaming villagers blowing horns and banging drums. This was repeated for three successive nights, the leader of the 'stang' reciting a piece of doggerel that had been specially written for the offender. The last person to 'Ride the Stang' was Joseph Pickard, a former landlord of the 'Fox and Hounds.' He had a fiery temper and had to face this ridicule for beating his wife.

From West Burton a line of gap-stiles leads through the fields and onto a quiet, tree-shaded lane. The delightful hamlet of

Newbiggin is within easy reach, so why not take a quick peep?

During the 1800s the community of Newbiggin consisted of leadminers who worked on Wasset Fell, three tailors, a cobbler, two shopkeepers and a smith. At the centre of the hamlet, near the bridge, there is an old sheep-fold and sheep-wash. Sheep washing, an annual event, took place in mid June and signalled the start of three days of fun and feasting. The event was known as the Newbiggin Feast and ended with the First World War.

Across the valley is the quiet farming village of Thoralby, which nestles on the southern slopes surrounded by flower-rich meadows, woodland and pastures. The village is recorded in Domesday Book as 'Turoldesbi,' its name means 'Thorold's Farm.' It has a small triangular green enclosed by stone built cottages, a village hall and an eighteenth-century inn. Thoralby folk used to say that Newbiggin was on the 'money side,' while they were on the 'sunny side'.

Leaving Newbiggin our route leads up to the conifer plantation at Forelands Rigg where we follow the ridge towards Wasset Fell before descending through the woodland into the lovely, sequestered valley of Walden. The name, meaning 'the valley of the foreigners,' applies to the whole dale, although it is sometimes incorrectly referred to as Waldendale or the Walden Valley. Academics would argue that the latter names were tautologically incorrect. The suffix 'den' and 'dale' both mean 'valley', therefore they would mean 'the valley of the valley of the foreigners'.

With Buckden Pike at its head the dale was prevented from having its own glacier and Walden was created by water erosion, resulting in its steep V-shape. The only way in or out of the valley, unless on foot, is via West Burton. In the fourteenth century, when red deer roamed throughout most of Wensleydale, Walden was made into a hunting reserve together with Bishopdale and Penhill. It was also one of the last refuges in Yorkshire for the wild cat and the pine marten. Walden is now designated as an Environmentally Sensitive Area and the use of traditional farming methods is encouraged. This helps to stimulate the growth of wild flowers, which in their turn attract a variety of butterflies, birds and small mammals to the area.

Our walk continues down the valley between the slopes of Penhill and Wassett Fell, with Walden Beck sparkling below. After passing through numerous meadows to Cote Bridge we follow the beck downstream to Blue Bridge, an ancient packhorse bridge, where the striking Cauldron Falls make a memorable finale to the walk.

| | |
|---|---|
| **Start/Parking:** | West Burton, park along the road around the village green. |
| **Location:** | West Burton is situated 8 miles (12.8km) west of Leyburn on the B6160 Kettlewell and Skipton road. |
| **Grid Ref:** | SE 017 866. |
| **Distance:** | $6\frac{1}{4}$ miles (10.1km) circular. Allow 3 hrs walking time. |
| **Total Ascent:** | 1206 feet (369m) Maximum Elevation: 1336 feet 407m). |
| **OS Maps:** | Explorer OL30 (1:25,000) or Landranger 98 (1:50,000). |
| **Refreshments:** | The Fox and Hounds at West Burton,<br>The Street Head Inn at Newbiggin,<br>The George Inn at Thoralby. |
| **Public Toilets:** | None *en route*, nearest Aysgarth Falls. |
| **Other:** | Post Office, bus service, shops, telephone. |

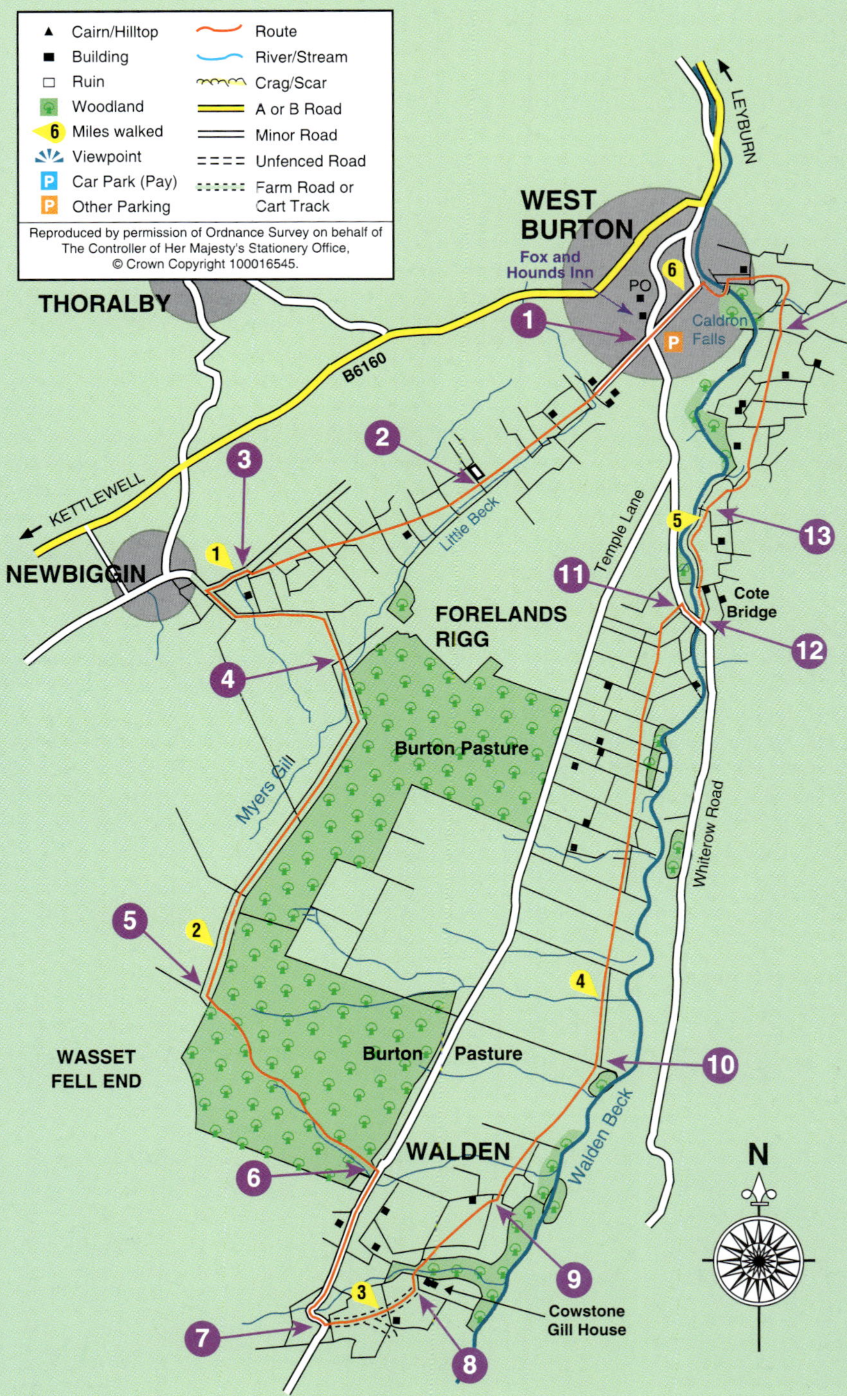
Cairn/Hilltop
Building
Ruin
Woodland
Miles walked
Viewpoint
Car Park (Pay)
Other Parking
Route
River/Stream
Crag/Scar
A or B Road
Minor Road
Unfenced Road
Farm Road or Cart Track
Reproduced by permission of Ordnance Survey on behalf of The Controller of Her Majesty's Stationery Office, © Crown Copyright 100016545.
LEYBURN
WEST BURTON
Fox and Hounds Inn
PO
Caldron Falls
THORALBY
B6160
KETTLEWELL
NEWBIGGIN
Little Beck
Temple Lane
FORELANDS RIGG
Cote Bridge
Burton Pasture
Myers Gill
Whiterow Road
WASSET FELL END
Burton Pasture
Walden Beck
WALDEN
Cowstone Gill House
N

# FORELANDS RIGG AND WALDEN BECK

**1** *(GR 017 866)* Walk to the top of the village, at the road junction continue uphill and go past the village hall. The lane begins to narrow and arrives at a farm. Go through the gate *(SP Newbiggin 1)* and cross a footbridge to the right. Continue on a clear path through several gap-stiles and a broken wall to a ruined barn.

**2** *(GR 011 861)* Cross the stile to the left of the barn *(SP Newbiggin)* and continue via a further line of gap-stiles and broken walls, eventually emerging onto a farm lane.

**3** *(GR 003 858)* Turn left and follow the lane to a junction of tracks. Turn left and go through a gate. Continue on an enclosed track leading uphill and go through a gate. When the track becomes unenclosed, turn left and stay close to the left wall. Follow the wall round and climb up to the forestry plantation at Forelands Rigg.

**4** *(GR 006 855)* Join an enclosed track which passes between the plantation fence and a wall. Continue uphill and turn right along the side of the plantation. Follow the track over two wooden step-stiles, until a fence blocks further progress.

**5** *(GR 002 844)* Cross the wooden step-stile on the left to enter the plantation. Continue on a wide track which descends through the plantation and emerges onto a tarmacked lane.

**6** *(GR 008 838)* Turn right and follow the lane for about 600 yards (550m) crossing a small bridge and continue round a double bend.

**7** *(GR 006 833)* On the second part of the double bend leave the road through a gateway on the left *(SP Cote Bridge 1½)*. Follow the farm lane downhill. At a bend leave the lane, taking the left fork. Go over a cattle grid to the left of the barn and continue to Cowstone Gill House.

**8** *(GR 009 834)* Go along a track to the left of the farmhouse *(SP West Burton)*. Continue through a gap-stile and cross the footbridge over Cowstone Gill. Go through a gate and climb up to a fence. Cross a wooden step-stile and head to the far right corner of the field to cross another wooden step-stile.

**9** *(GR 011 835)* Turn left, go through two gap-stiles and then follow a line of waymark posts through rough pasture to the next gap-stile.

**10** *(GR 015 842)* Go through the stile and continue on an obvious path via another series of gap-stiles and gates to reach the road near Cote Bridge.

**11** *(GR 018 857)* Turn right and follow the road for about 30 yards (27m), crossing the bridge over Walden Beck.

**12** *(GR 018 856)* Leave the road via a gate on the left *(SP Rookwith Bridge ¼)*. Follow the beck downstream and go through a gate. Stay with the left wall and go through a gap-stile to reach Rookwith Bridge.

**13** *(GR 018 860)* Bear right to leave the beckside *(SP Riddings)*. Go through a gap-stile in the right-hand corner, turn left and follow the wall round to another gap-stile. Go through the stile and bear right. Follow a clear path through four gap-stiles passing the farmhouse at Riddings.

**14** *(GR 021 866)* Continue ahead and descend slightly to go through a gap-stile in the wall opposite. Cross a small stream and follow the wall to its corner. Turn left and follow the wall down through a stile to the left of a barn. Follow an enclosed path descending through a gate to reach the stone bridge over Walden Beck. Cross the bridge and turn right to return to West Burton village.

**Cauldron Falls are upstream from the bridge and they can be reached along paths on either side of Walden Beck.**

(SEPT 16) EXCELLENT. IN MY TOP 5! NEEDS A CLEAR DAY. START AT CREAMERY. SO CAN HAVE CHIPS COMING BACK THROUGH HAWES.

# 10

# HAWES, TEN END and GAYLE

## FROM HAWES 7¼ MILES (11.7KM)

**Starting from Hawes, the capital of Upper Wensleydale, this moderate hill walk follows two ancient tracks climbing to 1882 feet (574m). It provides panoramic views across the side valleys of Sleddale, Snaizeholme and Widdale.**

Hawes, standing at 850 feet (260m), is Yorkshire's highest market town with high fells to both north and south. Although it only received its charter in 1699, from William III, Hawes soon captured the trade of the established markets at Askrigg and Carperby. In 1795 a turnpike road to Lancaster was built enabling the larger, wheeled transport to compete with the pack-horse routes. This gave Hawes a significant advantage and its status as the capital of Upper Wensleydale was assured. The arrival of the railways in 1878 helped the town to expand further and stimulated the growth of local trades and industries. The old railway buildings are now used by the National Park as a visitor centre and they also house the Dales Countryside Museum.

The museum's unique collection was originally started in the 1940s by two local historians and writers, Marie Hartley and Ella Pontefract. They scoured the dales, attending auctions and farm sales in order to prevent objects from disappearing into oblivion. After Ella's death in 1945, Marie was joined by Joan Ingleby and together they continued the collection which led to the founding of the museum in 1979. The displays include a dales' kitchen, a doctor's surgery, a lead mine, farming implements and memorabilia, crafts and tools, helping to show what life in the dale was like in days gone by.

One of the old crafts can still be seen nearby. At Outhwaite's, the ropemakers, a

200 year-old method of hand twisting rope is used. Visitors can watch rope being twisted to make cattle halters, clothes lines and even dog leads.

Our route from the car park leads to the market place and then continues to the Wensleydale Creamery where the famous Wensleydale cheese is made.

There has been a creamery at Hawes since 1897. When it was threatened with closure in 1935, prompt action had to be taken. Kit Calvert, a well-known expert on the Wensleydale dialect, was opposed to the closure. He invested some capital himself and with the support of a co-operative of local farmers the creamery was rescued. The modern creamery has a visitor centre, viewing gallery, museum and specialist cheese shop. Wensleydale cheese was first made by Cistercian monks from Jervaulx Abbey. The original recipe used ewe's milk. In the 1300s cow's milk started to take over from ewe's and the character of the cheese began to change. The cheese is still matured using traditional methods.

We leave Hawes opposite the creamery and after a short walk through the fields we join the Cam Road and begin a gradual climb to Ten End.

The Cam Road is an old drove road from Hawes to Horton-in-Ribblesdale. As the industrial towns grew in size, the demand for fresh meat also increased. Drove roads were established to bring thousands of cattle and sheep from the Scottish Highlands. Drovers became an important link between towns. Wealthy merchants trusted them to take money to pay bills in other towns. To avoid the risk of robbery, the drover left the money at home and paid the bill from the sale of cattle, 'gold on the hoof'.

At Ten End we join the Pennine Way and the climbing is over. Below lies the sequestered valley of Snaizeholme and, looking towards the dale head, the bold outlines of Ingleborough and Whernside loom. During our descent to Gayle there is a wonderful panorama of Wensleydale and Sleddale.

Gayle is a charming village, founded by the Vikings as a summer farm; evidence has also shown the existence of an earlier Iron Age settlement. The beck, rising on Dodd Fell, cascades over a series of limestone ledges splitting the village in two. The main industry in Gayle was hand-knitting; whole families were involved in the knitting of hats, stockings and jerseys.

From Gayle our route heads across the fields to the Hawes auction mart. Regular livestock sales are held here, handling over 100,000 sheep and 12,000 cattle each year. The sales are exciting affairs for spectators, but take care, as scratching your nose at the wrong time could mean you have become the proud new owner of a few shearlings!

From the auction mart we return to the main road, which is followed back to the car park.

| | |
|---|---|
| **Start/Parking:** | The Hawes National Park Visitor Centre has a large car park. Parking is also available in a car park behind the school just off the Gayle road. |
| **Location:** | Hawes is situated 15 miles (24km) east of Sedburgh on the A684 Northallerton to Sedburgh road. |
| **Grid Ref:** | SD 875 898. |
| **Distance:** | 7¼ miles (11.7km) circular. Allow 3½ hrs walking time. |
| **Total Ascent:** | 1283 feet (392m) Maximum Elevation: 1882 feet (574m) |
| **OS Maps:** | Explorer OL30 or OL2 (1:25,000) or Landranger 98 (1:50,000). |
| **Refreshments:** | Several inns, cafes, tea rooms and a fish shop at Hawes. |
| **Public Toilets:** | Hawes National Park Visitor Centre and the market place. |
| **Other:** | Post Office, shops, telephone, bus service. |

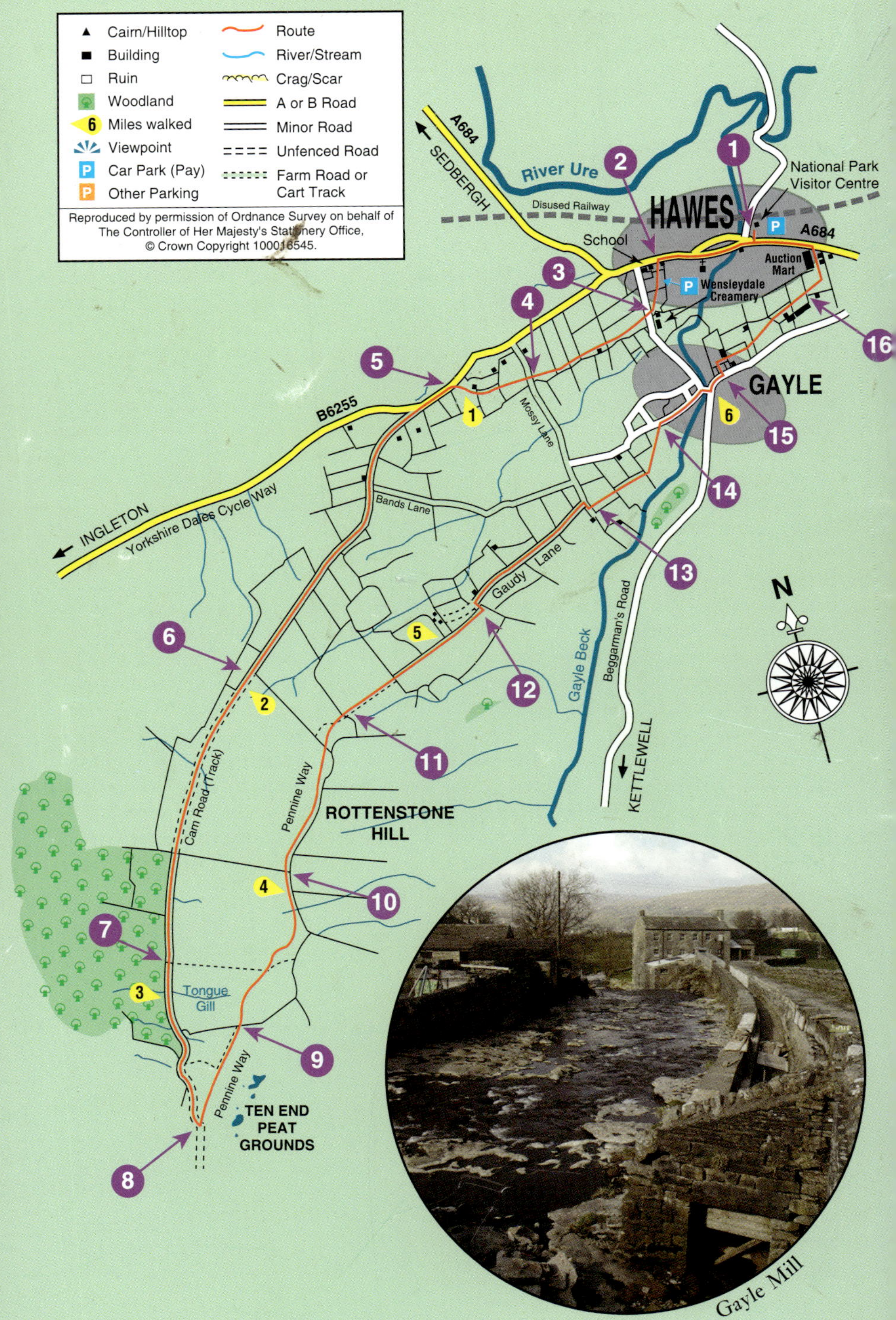
Cairn/Hilltop
Building
Ruin
Woodland
6 Miles walked
Viewpoint
Car Park (Pay)
Other Parking
Route
River/Stream
Crag/Scar
A or B Road
Minor Road
Unfenced Road
Farm Road or Cart Track
Reproduced by permission of Ordnance Survey on behalf of The Controller of Her Majesty's Stationery Office, © Crown Copyright 100016545.
A684
SEDBERGH
River Ure
Disused Railway
HAWES
National Park Visitor Centre
A684
School
Auction Mart
Wensleydale Creamery
GAYLE
B6255
Mossy Lane
Bands Lane
INGLETON
Yorkshire Dales Cycle Way
Gaudy Lane
Gayle Beck
Beggarman's Road
KETTLEWELL
N
Cam Road (Track)
Pennine Way
ROTTENSTONE HILL
Tongue Gill
Pennine Way
TEN END PEAT GROUNDS
1
2
3
4
5
6
7
8
9
10
11
12
13
14
15
16
Gayle Mill

# Hawes, Ten End and Gayle

**1** *(GR 875 898)* Return to the car park entrance and cross over the main road. Turn right and follow the road through the village passing over Gayle Beck and through the market square.

**2** *(GR 871 898)* After passing the Market Hall turn left into a small car park. Climb some steps in the left corner *(SP Gayle Lane)* and continue up the path into another car park. Follow a narrow path round and through a gap-stile. Bear right across the field and go through a gap-stile onto the road near the Wensleydale Creamery.

**3** *(GR 870 896)* Cross the road and continue between the houses *(SP Mossy Lane ⅓)*. Climb up through a gap-stile in the left corner of the field and then follow a clear path across four more fields to reach Mossy Lane.

**4** *(GR 865 895* Cross the lane, go through the gap-stile opposite and continue across two fields to a derelict barn. Bear right and pass over a small hill to a gap-stile leading onto the B6255.

**5** *(GR 861 896)* Turn left and follow the road for about 100 yards (91m). At a bend leave the road along the rough enclosed track on the left and begin a steep climb that eventually arrives at a gate.

**6** *(GR 850 886)* Go through the gate where the track levels out slightly and becomes unenclosed. At the next gate the track becomes enclosed again and the surface begins to get rougher. Continue along the track by the side of the forestry plantation.

**7** *(GR 843 876)* Go through the gate and begin climbing more steeply. At the end of the forestry plantation the track becomes unenclosed. Continue along the track to a cairn *(SP Pennine Way)*.

**8** *(GR 843 869)* This is Ten End where the Pennine Way footpath is joined. Turn left here and follow a cairned path keeping to the right of a derelict wall.

**9** *(GR 846 872)* Go through the gate and begin a gradual descent, passing over a derelict wall and going through a gate.

**10** *(GR 849 878)* Follow the right wall and continue descending through a large pasture. Go through a gate and climbing up slightly, pass through a derelict wall near a cairn and continue through a gate.

**11** *(GR 853 884)* Follow the derelict right wall down through another gate. Then follow the left wall past Gaudy Farmhouse to a gate/stile.

**12** *(GR 860 887)* The gate leads onto Gaudy Lane. Turn right and follow the lane downhill to a T-Junction. At the T-Junction turn right for about 20 yards (18m).

**13** *(GR 865 889)* Leave the lane via a gap-stile on the left *(SP Pennine Way)*. Continue through two more gap-stiles. Head diagonally left across the field, pass a wall corner and descend to a metal kissing-gate which leads down a few steps onto a tarmacked lane.

**14** *(GR 869 893)* Turn right and follow the lane into Gayle. Turn right, cross the bridge and immediately turn left following the road towards Burtersett.

**15** *(GR 872 893)* Follow the lane for about 50 yards (46m). After passing East House leave the lane via a gate at the side of a cattle grid. Go through another gate, turn right and go through a gap-stile behind the barn/shed. Continue via a line of gap-stiles to arrive at the auction mart.

**16** *(GR 876 895)* The stile into the auction mart enters a livestock pen. Leave the pen and continue through the auction mart to the main road. Turn left and follow the road back to the car park.

# Glossary

Most of the local place-names are Anglo-Saxon or Norse in origin. They were made up from words used in everyday speech and described one particular spot, clearly defining it from other places in the immediate neighbourhood. Anglo-Saxon names include those ending with *ing, ley, ham* and *ton.* Norse names include those ending with *by, sett* and *thwaite.* The Normans had a smaller influence on place-names, being confined to changes in the spelling of existing names. They gave us the Domesday Book in 1086 recording the name, population and value of each village.

**Abbotside:** *The abbot's hill.*

**Addlebrough:** *Authulf's fort.*

**Appersett:** *The shieling near the apple tree.*

**Askrigg:** *The ash ridge.*

**Aysgarth:** *The open space in the oak trees.*

**Bailey:** *A forecourt surrounded by an earth rampart.*

**Bain, river:** *The straight river.*

**Bainbridge:** *The bridge over the river Bain.*

**Bear Park:** *The hill paddock.*

**Beck:** *Stream.*

**Bishopdale:** *Bishop's valley.*

**Braithwaite:** *The broad clearing.*

**Brough Hill:** *The fortification.*

**Burtersett:** *The shieling near the alder tree.*

**Caldbergh:** *The cold hill.*

**Cam Road:** *The road along the ridge.*

**Carperby:** *Cairpre's farm.*

**Castle Bolton:** *The village with buildings near the castle.*

**Cotescue:** *Scot's wood.*

**Cotterdale:** *The valley with the huts.*

**Countersett:** *Constance's shieling.*

**Cover, river:** *The river in a hollow.*

**Coverdale:** *The valley of the river Cover.*

**Coverham:** *The homestead on the river Cover.*

**Dodd Fell:** *The hill with the rounded top.*

**Gayle:** *The ravine.*

**Gill:** *A deep wooded ravine.*

**Hardraw:** *The shepherd's houses.*

**Hawes:** *The mountain pass.*

**Jervaulx:** *The Ure valley.*

**Keep:** *The chief inner tower of a castle.*

**Kidstones:** *The kid-goat stones.*

**Kilgram:** *Kelgrim's mound.*

**Kissing-gate:** *A gate hung in a V- or U-shaped enclosure allowing one person through at a time.*

**Leyburn:** *The stream by the clearing.*

**Lunds:** *The woods.*

**Marsett:** *Maurr's shieling.*

**Middleham:** *The middle homestead.*

**Mossdale:** *The boggy valley.*

**Motte:** *A mound with a flattened top on which a Norman fort stood.*

**Newbiggin:** *The new building.*

**Penhill:** *The hill.*

**Raydale:** *Roebuck Valley.*

**Redmire:** *The reed pool.*

**Shearling:** *A sheep that has been shorn once.*

**Shieling:** *A farm or summer pasture.*

**Shunner Fell:** *Sjon's hill.*

**Sleddale:** *The wide valley.*

**Snaizeholme:** *The twigs.*

**Stake Pass:** *The pass marked by stakes.*

**Stalling Busk:** *The stallion's bush.*

**Stony Raise:** *The stone cairn.*

**Thoralby:** *Thorold's farm.*

**Thornton Rust:** *Roschil's farm by the thorns.*

**Ulshaw:** *Ulf's mound.*

**Ure, river:** *The strong river.*

**Walden:** *The valley of the foreigners.*

**Wensley:** *Waendel's forest clearing.*

**West Burton:** *The fortified farmstead.*

**Widdale:** *The wooded valley.*

**Woodhall:** *The hall in the wood.*

**Worton:** *The vegetable garden.*

# The Country Code

Enjoy the countryside and respect its life and works

Keep to public paths across farmland

Leave livestock, crops and farm machinery alone

Use gates and stiles to cross fences, hedges and walls

Guard against all risks of fire

Make no unnecessary noise

Leave all gates as you find them

Take your litter home

Help to keep all water clean

Protect wildlife, plants and trees

Take special care on country roads

Keep dogs under close control

## Also . . .

Use car parks where possible and park with consideration for village residents and other road users.

Don't obstruct farm gates, tracks or entrances.

When walking on roads, walk on the right hand side to face oncoming traffic. When approaching blind bends, cross to the opposite side to enable you to see and be seen in both directions.

Allow sufficient time to complete the walk in daylight hours, and be sure to be off the fells by dusk.

Let others know the route you have taken, the time you expect to return and stick to the route.

If the weather turns nasty and you decide to quit the walk or take shelter in a hostelry etc, be sure to let others know so they do not worry and call out the emergency services unnecessarily.

# Information Desk

## ABBEYS

**Jervaulx Abbey,** between Middleham/Masham.
*A twelfth-century Cistercian abbey, although severely damaged at the dissolution it still has some graceful arches, pillars and carved stones.*

## CASTLES

**Bolton Castle,** Castle Bolton.
*This mighty fortress was built in 1379 for Richard le Scrope, Lord Chancellor of England to Richard II. Mary, Queen of Scots, was held here 'in honourable custody' during 1568 and 1569.*

**Middleham Castle,** Middleham
*The childhood and favourite home of Richard III, Middleham Castle once controlled the upper reaches of Wensleydale and Coverdale. It was built in the twelfth century and its central keep, one of the largest in England, has magnificent views of the surrounding countryside. (English Heritage)*

## FARM VISITS

**Big Sheep & Little Cow Farm,** Nr Bedale.
*Bottle feed hungry lambs, calves and piglets. Bath a pig, feed the cows and sheep, hold a variety of small animals and talk to the donkey.*

**Working Sheepdog Demonstrations,** Hawes.
*Local farmer and sheepdog trialist, Richard Fawcett, demonstrates his, and his dog's sheep handling skills. The dogs are amazing as they round up flocks of sheep at the mere whistle of the farmer.*

## HISTORIC HOUSES and GARDENS

**Braithwaite Hall, Nr** East Witton/Coverham.
*A seventeenth-century manor house which is also a working farm. This charming house has some fine original features including fireplaces and panelling. The main hall, sitting room and oak staircase are on show to visitors. (National Trust)*

**Constable Burton Hall,** Nr Leyburn.
*This large, romantic garden is surrounded by parkland with a superb Georgian house built by John Carr. Fine woodland walks combine with a collection of alpines and extensive shrubs and roses. Visit the stream garden with its large architectural plants and reflection ponds.*

**Edwardian Rock Garden,** Aysgarth.
*An amazing rock garden, which remained hidden for almost half a century. Some rare plants survive and there is a lovely atmosphere of eccentric grandeur of an earlier age.*

**Thorpe Perrow Arboretum & Falconry Centre,** Bedale.
*Woodland walks, tea room, plant centre, play area and picnic area. Educational trails and many events. Largest display of birds of prey in the North. Captive breeding and conservation centre. Visitors have the opportunity to learn more about birds of prey, with the enjoyment of hands on experience for all the family.*

## MARKET DAYS

**Bedale,** Tuesday.
**Hawes,** Tuesday.
**Leyburn,** Friday.
**Masham,** Wednesday.

## MUSEUMS

**Bedale Hall Museum,** Bedale.
*Museum of local history containing items from Bedale and district from prehistoric times to the present day.*

**Crakehall Water Mill,** Little Crakehall, Bedale
*A working, water corn mill. tea room, ice cream parlour and a museum of agricultural bygones.*

**The Dales Countryside Museum,** Hawes.
*Exhibitions of life on a dale's farm, hand-knitting, cheese-making, country crafts and much more.*

**Low Mill,** Bainbridge.
*Working watermill, recently restored.*

## NATURAL FEATURES

**Aysgarth Falls,** Aysgarth Falls.
*Aysgarth Falls are a delight at any time of the year, but when in spate they are magnificent.*

**Bain Falls,** Bainbridge.
*Situated on England's shortest river, Bain Falls form a broad crescent shape, spectacular after heavy rain.*

**Hardraw Force (or Scaur),** Hardraw.
*England's highest unbroken waterfall comprising a single drop of 100 feet (30.5m) from a rocky overhang.*

**Semer Water,** Nr Bainbridge.
*Yorkshire's third largest lake. The lake is glacial in origin but it is also steeped in legend.*

## PETROL STATIONS

Aysgarth, Bedale, Hawes, Leyburn, Woodhall

## TOURIST INFORMATION POINTS

**Askrigg,** Post Office, Main Street.
**Aysgarth Falls,** National Park Visitor Centre.
**Bedale,** Bedale Hall, North End.
**Hawes,** National Park Visitor Centre.
**Hawes,** The Youth Hostel, Lancaster Terrace.
**Leyburn,** 4 Central Chambers.
**Masham,** Little Market Place.
**Thoralby,** Post Office, The Green.
**West Witton,** Withywood Stores, Main Street.

## VETERINARY SURGERIES

**Cupplesfield Veterinary Surgery,** Bainbridge.
**Forrest House Veterinary Group,** Bedale.
**Hollin Rigg Veterinary Surgery,** Leyburn.
**Linscott & Best,** Bedale, Leyburn and Masham.

## YOUTH HOSTELS

**Bishopdale Valley Bunkhouse,** Nr Aysgarth.
**Hawes,** Lancaster Terrace, Hawes.